CAMPFIRE STORIES

CAMPFIRE STORIES

Tales from
America's National Parks

Edited by
Dave Kyu and Ilyssa Kyu

MOUNTAINEERS
BOOKS

MOUNTAINEERS BOOKS is the publishing division of The Mountaineers, an organization founded in 1906 and dedicated to the exploration, preservation, and enjoyment of outdoor and wilderness areas.

1001 SW Klickitat Way, Suite 201, Seattle, WA 98134
800-553-4453, www.mountaineersbooks.org

Printed in Canada
Distributed in the United Kingdom by Cordee, www.cordee.co.uk
24 23 22 21   6 7 8 9 10

Copyeditor: Laura Lancaster
Design and layout: Melissa McFeeters
Illustration on pages 22 – 23 © Allison May Kiphuth; illustration on pages 58 – 59 © Sarah Jacoby; illustration on pages 92 – 93 © Emily Dove; illustration on pages 138 – 139 © Maggie Chiang; illustration on pages 166 – 167 © Josie Portillo; illustration on pages 200 – 201 © Zoe Keller

Library of Congress Cataloging-in-Publication Data
Names: Kyu, Dave, editor of compilation. | Kyu, Ilyssa, editor of compilation.
Title: Campfire stories : tales from America's National Parks / edited by Dave Kyu and Ilyssa Kyu.
Other titles: Tales from America's National Parks
Description: Seattle, WA : Mountaineers Books, [2018] | Includes bibliographical references.
Identifiers: LCCN 2018015725| ISBN 9781680511444 (hardcover) | ISBN 9781680511451 (ebook)
Subjects: LCSH: Campfire programs. | National parks and reserves—United States--Folklore. | Indians of North America—Folklore. | Tales—United States. | Storytelling—United States. | Nature in literature.
Classification: LCC GV198.R4 C36 2018 | DDC 796.54/5—dc23
LC record available at https://lccn.loc.gov/2018015725

Mountaineers Books titles may be purchased for corporate, educational, or other promotional sales, and our authors are available for a wide range of events. For information on special discounts or booking an author, contact our customer service at 800-553-4453 or mbooks@mountaineersbooks.org.

Printed on FSC-certified materials

ISBN (hardcover): 978-1-68051-144-4

For our little stowaway,
Lula June

Contents

ACADIA NATIONAL PARK
An Island on the Sea

GREAT SMOKY MOUNTAINS NATIONAL PARK
Home in the Mountains of Blue Smoke

ROCKY MOUNTAIN NATIONAL PARK
A Place for the Wild

ZION NATIONAL PARK
A Sanctuary in the Desert

YOSEMITE NATIONAL PARK
A Cathedral of Granite

YELLOWSTONE NATIONAL PARK
A Storied Wonderland

MAY YOUR TRAILS BE CROOKED, winding, lonesome, dangerous, leading to the most amazing view. May your mountains rise into and above the clouds. May your rivers flow without end, meandering through pastoral valleys tinkling with bells, past temples and castles and poets' towers into a dark primeval forest where tigers belch and monkeys howl, through miasmal and mysterious swamps and down into a desert of red rock, blue mesas, domes and pinnacles and grottoes of endless stone, and down again into a deep vast ancient unknown chasm where bars of sunlight blaze on profiled cliffs, where deer walk across the white sand beaches, where storms come and go as lightning clangs upon the high crags, where something strange and more beautiful and more full of wonder than your deepest dreams waits for you—beyond that next turning of the canyon walls.

So long.

Benedictio
—Edward Abbey

Foreword

I AM AN ACCIDENTAL NATIONAL PARKS ADVOCATE. There are 417 national park sites in the United States covering some 84 million acres. But before 2004, I hadn't really thought about them. I had taken a road trip from Washington State to Minnesota in a VW bus with an old boyfriend back in the mid-nineties and had eaten too many hotdogs and marshmallows around a campfire in Yellowstone, but while I enjoyed the scenery (and the hotdogs), back then I didn't think much about it beyond my singular experience of vacationing on these public lands.

Things changed for me in 2008 when I was asked to serve on the Second Century Commission and subsequently, the National Parks Advisory Board. Due to my role as a scholar and writer working on issues related to diversity and public engagement, the National Parks Service believed that my thoughts and ideas would be useful in developing better relationships with diverse communities.

My passion is for those stories of people and places and histories that are relegated to the margins of the larger narrative of who we are as Americans and as human beings on this land. But as an African American woman who is acutely aware of how some stories of our past are obscured or forgotten, particularly those that reveal the many ways we have demeaned, devalued, and dismissed those considered "different," I realized I had something personal at stake. Stories can tell us who we are and who we can be. Stories are how we make sense of the world and how we tell the world that we are here. Stories are a way to connect to the past and to each other. And stories are a way to signal that we belong. I wanted to see myself in those stories.

As I traveled around the country during the eight years I served, visiting numerous national parks as part of my advisory board experience, I saw so many stories on the landscape, heard them from park rangers whose story-telling skills were surpassed only by the stories themselves—tales that could barely be contained by words alone. I felt those stories in my bones the way you feel something that you didn't know was there but that is also at once familiar. Simply put, I was moved in a way that was unexpected and revelatory. And for the first time I understood that our national parks are a living repository of the stories of our lives.

In these pages, there are writers—there are *people*—whose lives and experiences and stories explore the different ways we all see and feel the world. While their points of reference and points of view reveal differences that some of us might not recognize or even agree with, what the storytellers share is a vitality of living, loving, dreaming, and showing up in these outdoor spaces that continue to hold us and tell us who we are.

So, grab your marshmallow sticks, find a comfortable place to sit, and open up to the voices and hearts of the storytellers in these pages. The magic is here for the taking. Once upon a time . . .

—*Carolyn Finney*
author of *Black Faces, White Spaces: Reimagining the Relationship of African Americans to the Great Outdoors*

Introduction

THE CRACKLE OF THE FIRE, the chirp of crickets hanging in the air. The campfire is the rare setting in a modern world where distractions fade away, leaving only those sharing the flickering light with you. But what if you don't know any good stories? If you're like us, two lifelong Philadelphians with a budding interest in the outdoors, you might drop everything to travel the country to find those stories. This book is the culmination of a cross-country search for stories to share around a fire, from America's favorite national parks.

We live in an age of storytelling. Writers of television, film, and podcasts are sharing stories with wonderful complexity and unprecedented production value. In the digital age, we are reading more news, opinion, and think pieces than ever. We're even writing our personal stories to share through social media. We've never been hungrier to tell or hear a good story. So when the two of us started this journey, our first question was, "What's your favorite story about this place?" Yet, the response we got most often was, "I don't know any." That's exactly where we started, with this sentiment that inspired this book. Because today, we're all surrounded by great narratives, but we don't feel they are ours to tell.

This book was born, naturally, around a campfire. One evening in Acadia National Park in Maine, watching the embers float into the dark night sky, we found ourselves inadvertently reaching for our phones—the millennial cure for a silent moment. Neither of us had grown up with family camping trips; in fact, we discovered camping by accident. Years ago, just before leaving for a week's vacation in Toronto, the city's sanitation workers went on strike. Stacks of garbage shut down the city—in some neighborhoods, as high as the fences of the local basketball courts. When a friend suggested that we instead drive up US Route 1, along the New England coast, ending in Acadia National Park, we thought, "Why not?" We spent the week rambling through the cozy main streets of charming New England towns, and arrived at Acadia to camp for the first time as adults. That first night, we struggled to set up our tent and slept directly on the ground, shivering through the night when the granite sucked all the heat out of our bodies. But we fell in love with the Maine coast anyway. We've gone back to Acadia every year for the past decade.

We were hooked. We found that being outdoors replenished our souls in a way that we hadn't even known to look for. We started planning our trips, not to cities, but to spend time in the great outdoors. Weekends, time off, sick days: we squeezed nature into all the margins of our life, and found there was always more to discover. Which made it that much more alarming when we reached for our phones that one night around a campfire. We felt compelled to correct that impulse.

The plan for *Campfire Stories* wasn't always to travel. Plan A was to find an existing collection of stories, order it with two-day shipping, and give it as a nice gift. End of story. But we found only collections of spooky ghost stories. Plan B was only slightly more ambitious. We went to the local library and checked out collections of folklore, expecting to pick out our favorites. Instead, as we dove into these collections, we found ourselves asking: what makes one story better than another? Which ones were true, and which ones were half-true? Which regional stories accurately and authentically depicted a place, its history, or its culture? And who were we to select any one story over another?

Armed with curiosity, we thought back to our first trip to Acadia, and how vital it was to have a map to guide us, a bathroom, and a shower nearby. These amenities gently eased us newcomers into connecting with nature. National parks, we decided, were perfect introductions for those with limited experience in wild places: not completely cut off from modern amenities, but not quite civilized either. Knowing it was the National Park Service's one hundredth anniversary, we thought there was no better way to celebrate and honor its history than to seek out and tell its story to a broad audience. To tell the true and authentic stories of America's favorite national parks, we needed to hit the road.

We mapped out a route that gave us two weeks each in six national parks. In each park, we reached out to park rangers and "friends of" groups, as well as libraries, museums, tribal representatives, historical societies, arts and cultural organizations, business owners, and long-time residents in the nearby communities. Each conversation quite literally led us to the next, and provided a better understanding of which stories to look for, and, just as important, which to avoid. We stitched together their diverse points of view with our own experiences of each national park to create a loose rubric for stories that capture the complex, nuanced, and emotional story of place. This process was vital for us to responsibly select the stories in this collection. It wasn't a historic, scientific, or even a traditional folklorist's process—it was our own journey of a lifetime: four months spent living out of a car, going from state to state, and looking to understand the America that we live in today through the stories we continue to tell.

This book is organized in the order of the parks we've visited. First is Acadia, the park where we figured out how this "fishing expedition" might work. Then it was off to the lush hollows of the Great Smoky Mountains—the park where we learned an unexpected stowaway (Wait, we're pregnant?! Now?!) would make for a very different road trip! In the Rocky Mountains, we learned how hard people fight for their water, and, at 7,000 feet above sea level, that lip balm really is the sidearm of the West. We struggled to adapt to the arid desert of Zion in Utah, right in the middle of a heat wave, but came to appreciate the sparseness of the landscape through the stories we uncovered. Yet, we still rushed to the California coast for respite alongside the Pacific Ocean, before moving on to the broad valleys and green meadows of Yosemite, for which the famous naturalist John Muir fell head over heels. And we ended our trip where the whole idea of America's parks began, in the wonderland of Yellowstone.

Millions of Americans visit national parks each year, and create just as many special relationships with these places. In celebrating its one hundredth year, the National Park Service kicked off the Find Your Park campaign, a challenge not just to reflect on the first century of parks, but to look forward to the next one hundred years. As we traveled, we kept the Park Service's call to look forward close to our hearts. We noted how the story of the national parks was told by only a few voices, and how often offensive parlance appeared in early texts. We reminded ourselves that all national park lands were once home to American Indians. We sought out the perspectives of the female naturalists and pioneers who were vital in helping to shape the park system. For our team of two, Korean-American and Jewish, husband and wife, it was important for us to find stories that could widen the lens of who our public lands are for.

We know that stories can achieve this. Stories can play a powerful role in creating the emotional connections necessary to create individual bonds with nature. They teach lessons, build empathy, and share ideas that are important to the art of living. Whether you are reading this book around a campfire, in your living room, at your local park, or beside a child's bed, we hope you will find something that makes nature come alive. This is especially true for younger generations, who are increasingly disconnected from the outdoors, and who, one day, will be responsible for protecting it.

This book is our search for those great campfire stories. The poems, ballads, legends, songs, short stories, myths, and essays herein have been collected through countless interviews with individuals who live and work in and around six of America's favorite national parks. Each and every park could fill volumes, and so we hope you'll peruse this small sample of entertaining yarns we've assembled, and look to our sources to learn more about any particular topic. We hope these stories capture the diverse history, cultures, and experiences of those who have collectively built, shared, and enjoyed these parks across the country. We hope reading or telling these stories will evoke the camaraderie that can be found inside a good campfire story. We hope these stories will reignite our imagination about the wild.

Storytelling Tips

THE FOLLOWING HINTS FOR READING THESE STORIES ALOUD around a campfire were developed in conversation with Benjamin Camp, Artistic Director for Team Sunshine Performance Corporation, a Philadelphia-based theater and dance company. In addition to having "Camp" as a last name, Benjamin is uniquely suited for campfire story magic-making after his love of attending camp as a kid and camp counselor led him to cofound and direct Camp Bonfire, a summer camp for adults in the northeastern United States. Whether you just need a refresher, or you've never read aloud at a campfire, these suggestions should get you ready.

Keep in mind, these tips are here to serve as a loose guide. Find what works for you and your audience, and know that you won't be on the spot. A campfire is a perfect place for someone to watch the fire or look at the stars, and not directly at you. Have a sip of water, share the things about a story that you love, keep it simple, and relax. Remember that you're sharing a beautiful campfire with a group of people, and a reading will just enhance this memorable experience.

Choose the right story.

A crucial part of telling a good campfire story is selecting the right story for your audience. Think about whose attention you need to hold, and what they might be interested in. For example, children might be more interested in a bear story than a reflective memoir about geology. Think also about the length of your story. Is this one of many activities or are you settled in for the night? Are you reading to kids with short attention spans or a group of engaged adults? Choosing a story that's too long is a common rookie mistake.

Read it out loud ahead of time.

Don't think of it as practice; reading ahead simply allows you to feel more relaxed later. Reading out loud in advance will reveal the words you can't pronounce, and will give you time to look up words you don't know. For the overachievers who want to memorize or perform the story, reading out loud often helps you memorize better than reading internally.

Set yourself up for a good reading.

Water is magic for any voice. Having water on hand can rescue you from dry mouth or a fit of coughing. Remember that, in a camp setting, you are competing with the chirping of crickets and the crackle of the fire. Make sure you sit or stand straight up, breathe from your diaphragm, and project your voice. As you're reading, don't forget to breathe or you might find yourself gasping for air.

Bring a flashlight.

The campfire provides a warm, flickering light that sets the perfect mood. But if you're relying on this light to read your book, you're also probably projecting your voice away from your intended audience. We recommend bringing a flashlight so you can read to your audience, and still see the text. If you want to go hands-free, bring a headlamp or a book light that can clip onto the book.

Wait for the right moment to start.

You want to start from a beautiful, perfect silence. If people are fiddling with their sleeping bags or rooting around in the cooler for their favorite drink, it's not the right time. There's a moment when the audience is ready—they are captive, silent, and all breathing together. This is when you want to begin. Don't miss it!

Introduce the story.

But keep it short and sweet. Share the title, author, and the park the story pertains to. If the story is written in the first person, you might share a bit of info about the author. Feel free to borrow a little insider knowledge from the accompanying "About This Story" blurb to get your audience excited!

Find the rhythm—and then break it.

A good performer establishes a rhythm, and then breaks it. Every story has its own rhythm, especially poetry. Stories read out loud should be read slightly faster than you think, but without rushing. Ignoring punctuation like semicolons and hyphens can help keep the momentum. You will want to find the story rhythm that works for you, and then play with it. The volume, speed, and tone of your voice all affect the rhythm of the story. If you can make the rhythm break surprising, this can be very fun for your listeners! A break in rhythm can include a silent pause, but use such pauses sparingly for greater effect.

Don't let performing get in the way.

You want to illustrate the story with your voice, but you don't want to overdo it by being too dramatic. One way to avoid this is to just be you—be authentic. Try to convey your experience with the story as you go. Don't be afraid to laugh, gasp, or ponder a thought. Funny voices are entertaining, but make sure it doesn't slow you down or cause you to lose your rhythm. Most importantly, enunciate and speak clearly.

Say thank you.

Give space at the end of the story. Leave a brief moment of silence by taking a deep breath before saying "The End." Thank your listeners for their attention and allow any reactions to the story to flow naturally. You can also gauge your audience's interest for another reading.

ACADIA NATIONAL PARK

An Island on the Sea

BURSTING WITH ROCKY COASTLINES,
lighthouses, lush forests, and brilliantly
colored foliage, Acadia National Park on
Mount Desert Island is a New England
coastline dream. This relatively small
park is packed with a diverse range of
experiences afforded by the ocean, lakes,
and forests that comprise it.

illustration by
ALLISON MAY KIPHUTH

Mount Desert Island, which sits just off the Maine coast in the Atlantic Ocean, is home to Acadia National Park. In fact, much of the island is dedicated park land, including many of the smaller islands surrounding it. Acadia's unique landscapes and iconic landmarks—the rocky cliffs, ocean, tides, sea foam, waves, fog, snow, fresh air, pine trees, and mountains—elicit a visceral connection to this constantly evolving island on the sea, one which draws us back, year after year.

Acadia National Park is our spiritual home.

It's where our love for the outdoors was born, and where our love as a couple grew. It's the muse for many ukulele songs (Sometimes when I lose my mind / I want to drive north where I can find / my head / my heart / my soul. To where the trees they dance with me / And the mountains move so quietly) and the source of endless memories—the starlit drive on the winding roads of Cadillac Mountain, the fiery orange moonrise over Frenchman Bay, the sound of crashing waves on our private nook in the rocks. It's where we go to feel whole again, to reset our bodies and minds for the year to come. And, of course, where we eat our weight in lobster rolls.

After nearly a decade of annual pilgrimages north, it made sense to begin our journey in Acadia, where the idea for *Campfire Stories* was born.

Already familiar with the park itself, we decided Acadia would be the perfect place to test out our research approach and refine our process for selecting stories. For the month of October, we explored unfamiliar edges of the island, intoxicated by the brilliant fall foliage. After weeks of camping, the temperatures dropped along with the autumn leaves. When our dog, Tuuli, figured out how to ask to sleep in the car each night, we knew it was time to move indoors. We upgraded to the floor of a barn on the more residential west side of Mount Desert Island, known as the "quiet side of the island," where every day we woke before the crack of dawn to clear out for the farm staff's daily meeting. This change in scenery became a pivotal part in our getting to know the community on the island.

Just below the surface of all interactions on Mount Desert Island is the tension between being "from here" or "from away." The island has a history of welcoming those "from away": from the "rusticators," the artists and journalists who popularized this island in the mid-1800s—to wealthy families taking up summer residence, and individuals who have decided to make Mount Desert Island their permanent home year-round. Being "from here" means descending from many generations of island dwellers, and continuing that legacy. Even those born on Mount Desert Island who've moved away for several years or decades before returning, can be considered "from away." The "from here" title is also earned by those who choose to embrace the island through its North Atlantic winters. But consider the Wabanaki, the American Indians who retreated to Mount Desert Island each summer for thousands of years before any European settlers arrived. From their perspective, the "from here," "from away" tension is comical.

There's a strong sense of identity and pride tied to what the land offers and how one earns a living on Mount Desert Island. Mainers who actively choose to call Mount Desert Island home find ways to make it work through self-sufficiency and toughness. Early trades were logging, quarry mining, and fishing, until these resources were depleted. Today, the land supports lobstermen and farmers, but the primary industry is tourism: thousands of visitors are welcomed to the island each summer.

An iconic genre of humor, quintessential to the stories from this region, was forged out of the traditional rough and rugged way-of-life. A classic Maine joke goes like this:

> A lobster fisherman named Charles dies, so his wife tells her son to go put in the obituary, "Charles died." The son goes to the newspaper and tells them his mother wants to submit the obituary as "Charles died." Since everyone knows Charles, that's enough. But the newspaperman says it has to be at least five words. The son goes back and tells his mother. She thinks for a minute and says, "Charles died. Boat for sale."

Maine humor elicits the resourcefulness of its people, and reflects a willingness to accept what this life has to offer—the good and the bad.

But despite the region's rugged facade, we discovered a wealth of warmth and generosity—from people giving up hours of their day to speak to us, helping to connect us with others, and sharing a little piece of their life by inviting us into their homes. One of the first sentiments shared was, "I would hope there would be stories that demonstrate the generosity and giving nature this park was founded on." Throughout our visit, we heard of many examples of this generosity—from people coming together to help out an ill member of the community to the history of how the park was first formed through the efforts of George Dorr, the "Father of Acadia."

George Dorr, a Harvard-educated, wealthy heir to a New England textile fortune, led the group crusade to form Acadia National Park in 1916. Back then, Acadia was the summer getaway of some of America's wealthiest families: the Roosevelts, the Rockefellers, the Pulitzers, the Fords. That legacy continues today, with famous Mount Desert Island residents like Martha Stewart, Susan Sarandon, and Stephen King. Dorr had the social connections necessary to coordinate the establishment, care, and expansion of the first park to be cobbled together entirely out of private land. As the park's first superintendent, Dorr ensured its sustainability by taking a salary of $1 per month. He spent his life and all his wealth to protect and share the beauty of this island—and by this devotion, overcame his "from away" status to become accepted as a native son, as someone "from here."

Our experience in Acadia not only refined our process for discovering stories, but also deepened our appreciation of an island we thought we knew so well.

Excerpt from
The Hour of Land

TERRY TEMPEST WILLIAMS

ay the word "Maine" and I swoon. It is everything my home in the American West is not. It is not wet. It is not green. Nor does it exist on the continent. Say the word "Acadia" and I see pink granite cliffs absorbing the shock of pounding waves, very different from the granite blocks I know that built the temple of my people in Salt Lake City. Say the words "Schoodic Point" and the taste of salt from the splash of tides reminds me of the inland sea that raised me in Utah's Great Basin.

"The edge of the sea is a strange and beautiful place," writes Rachel Carson.

It is here in "the settled wild" of Maine that I find sanctuary from the painful politics surrounding western wilderness. I don't know enough to have my heart broken in the east. What I do know is that over the past three decades I have been coming to Acadia National Park, this landscape has entered my DNA.

As the Colorado River shrinks from its historic banks due to drought, it is a comfort to sit on Acadia's Otter Cliff, a place of shimmering waters in the midst of a seeming apocalypse.

From a distance, the mountains in Acadia appear blue and rounded, not at all like the toothed peaks of the West with hanging canyons and glaciers. You can climb them in an afternoon, wearing a skirt. Their grandeur belongs not to ruggedness but to a gradual ascent toward grace. Once you're on top of the bald summit, a view of a watery planet inspires.

On my first trip to Maine I couldn't account for how familiar it felt—this place—this place where I had never been registered in my blood like heat. It didn't make sense. I didn't want to leave. I had to return.

It began with my aunt and uncle, Ruth and Richard Tempest, being called to serve on a mission for the Mormon Church in Cambridge, Massachusetts. Maine was part of their jurisdiction. While they were in church meetings on Sunday in Kennebunkport, my cousin Lynne and I would drive to the coast and explore.

Acadia National Park became a favorite haunt for our extended family. Our grandparents would stand on the edge of the continent looking east. It mattered to them, as westerners, to face Europe and remember both the sacrifices and courage of their ancestors and how they came west. Acadia became a tender point on the map for them. They said it reminded them of a time more genteel and predictable than the chaos and confusion of modern life.

For me, it became my secret respite. Here is where I come to meet my perfect solitude; where nothing is expected of me. There are times when the drama of the American West and Pacific Northwest exhausts me. We hear news that another grizzly bear has been killed in Yellowstone because they are afraid it is "a problem bear." Or another river has been fouled by an unexpected toxic spill from a spent gold mine, not far from Rocky Mountain National Park, or a coal train is going to be rerouted near North Cascades National Park in Washington.

This forested edge of the sea far, far away from the fossil fuel development in the American West shows us that what follows the story of destruction can be the story of restoration. The great fire of 1947 burned half of Mount Desert Island. Today, the woods are dense and lush. Maine's forests have been clear-cut and burned and cut again as recorded through photographs of the great Penobscot River choked with logs, eventually floating their way down to mill towns such as Bangor throughout the late nineteenth century. Timber and steel built America. Oil and gas are now fueling it.

My momentary retreats from my home ground in Utah allow me to breathe.

I love walking up Cadillac Mountain at dawn to see the sunrise, the first glint of light that appears in the United States from equinox to equinox. I love seeing the bodies of blue islands surface like whales at low tide and disappear at high, and the lobster buoys sprinkled over the waters like confetti. I love walking the rocky coast and finding brittle stars with outstretched legs crawling on wet, slippery rocks. I love how the sea anemones open and close like flowers with the inrushing tide. And I love retreating from the edge of the water into the damp woods soft with moss and fresh with fir. In the midst of birches and maples, lichen-drenched boulders in dappled light become the stage set for Noh Theater.

Acadia National Park is a cultural ecotone where civilization and wildness meet. In landscape ecology, an ecotone is defined as "the border area where two patches meet that have a different ecological composition." Think forest meets the ocean; meadow meets the woods; a desert becomes flush with a river. These edges create lines of tension. Call it a mete of creativity where the greatest diversity of species merge.

It is also a transition zone between those who leave and those who stay. In Maine there has always been tension between "summer people" and locals, where the human ecotone down east usually has to do with wealth—the lobstermen and clammers on one hand and the Astors and Rockefellers with their summer cottages on the other. In between, you have the nature lovers, or "rusticators," as they were called in the early twentieth century.

On a gently raining day, Brooke and I hike up Champlain Mountain, and as we do we imagine the era of rusticators not far removed from my grandparents had they lived here. We walk the stairs cut from granite so thoughtfully spaced, one after another, up the steep incline. We can envision the women lifting their long skirts so as not to slip on the rain-soaked stairs, now worn with time. It all feels so civilized. There is little delineation between sea and sky, only a soft gray-blue that folds into one graceful curve of cloud. The sound of foghorns guiding boats through rough water turns guttural. The rain stops and we eat our sandwiches on the summit. As we do, a stream of light breaks through the clouds. Below, a galaxy of stars dance on the Atlantic.

For all of us, Acadia is another breathing space. Perhaps that is what parks are—breathing spaces for a society that increasingly holds its breath. Here on the edge of the continent in this marriage between wind and sea, the weaving of currents offers a tapestry of relief.

Blue mussels, clam shells—broken and whole—slipper shells and limpets, lobster tails spent, buoys abandoned; a new world is at my feet. I wear an ankle bracelet of rockweed, bright yellow. A seal bobbing in the tide is watching.

Renascence—both the word and the poem by Edna St. Vincent Millay—return to me, the revival of something that has been dormant.

All I could see from where I stood
Was three long mountains and a wood;
I turned and looked another way,
And saw three islands in a bay.
So with my eyes I traced the line
Of the horizon, thin and fine,
Straight around till I was come
Back to where I'd started from;
And all I saw from where I stood
Was three long mountains and a wood.
Over these things I could not see;
These were the things that bounded me;
And I could touch them with my hand,
Almost, I thought, from where I stand.

Acadia National Park is personal for me. If Virginia Woolf speaks of a room of one's own, how about a place of one's own, not to be shared or spoken of except with the 2.5 million other visitors that come to Acadia each summer? I am not alone in my affections. In 2014, Acadia ranked as one of the top ten most popular national parks in America.

It is a privilege to visit Acadia, and it is privilege that has protected it. Established in 1916 as America's first national park east of the Mississippi (then known as Lafayette National Park), it was the first park to be created entirely out of private land and it is unique in that most of the land was donated. Every person associated with it acted out of love. Acadia's first superintendent, George B. Dorr, wealthy by inheritance, died virtually penniless, having given all he had to the cause of the park. Charles W. Eliot, president of Harvard, founded the Hancock County Trustees of Public Reservations to watch over it. And John D. Rockefeller Jr. donated more than eleven thousand acres of land to create it, and gave $3.5 million to support it. And then there were the carriage roads. This was Rockefeller's extraordinary obsession; a network of forty-five miles of roads meant only for horse-drawn carriages. Rockefeller wanted to make certain his beloved Mount Desert Island did not succumb to the automobile era (the irony that his fortune came from his family's ownership of Standard Oil and the advent of the automobile was not lost on him). He wanted to preserve a way of life that valued civility and slowness that he saw rapidly slipping away. Nostalgia in Maine is a virtue.

Between 1913 and 1940, Rockefeller saw these roads cut into green upholstered mountains, and curve around spruce and hemlock forests, and with each turn deliver yet another breathtaking view of the Atlantic.

The Park Service did not entirely appreciate Rockefeller's vision. They saw a system of roads at odds with protecting the wildlands of Mount Desert. Rockefeller saw it as another form of protection—protecting a way of life, and the peace that comes when time slows down and we venture into an aesthetic where nature and culture exist in harmony, not one without the other. And he saw the carriage roads as a way to open up the woods for those who may not be able to walk in the wilderness on their own. With a network of carriage roads, more people, the elderly included, could access the interior of the park. Rockefeller saw this as a democracy of experience, a way beyond privilege so that everyone could "own" these lands—a shared inheritance as American citizens.

As Horace M. Albright, director of the National Park Service from 1929 to 1933, said in Rockefeller's defense, "I believe Mr. Rockefeller had a genuine distaste for the garish advances of civilization . . . so he took every opportunity he felt possible to step in and save his fellow humans from the onslaught . . . of an industrial society."

A local told me that John D. Rockefeller Jr. said he spent so much money creating carriage roads throughout Acadia that he might as well have paved them with rubies. Last fall, I walked miles on one of his ruby-paved roads, red not from gemstones but from maple leaves. The path glistened from rain. Chipmunks and squirrels ran across the road with stuffed cheeks. Hermit thrushes foraged in the leaf litter, their spotted breasts becoming points of light in the elongated shadows of late afternoon. A kingfisher flew ahead, letting me know water was near. I left the road and entered the woods for a different point of view. In the canopy, a redstart snatched flies. I didn't know the underside of balsam fir looks like feathers, or of the deep, deep quiet that abides among these trees.

Back on the road, a wooden sign pointed to Aunt Betty's Pond. At the rate I was walking, stopping every few feet to look at a bird, a leaf, or an acorn, whether I would ever get to my destination was questionable. It was a six-mile meditation. There was no one else on the road. Up ahead, an orange pine needle hung twirling in the breeze—suspended from a high branch extended over the road from a single strand of spider's silk. The air was crisp, saturated with the scent of pine. All things were primary—red maples, yellow birch, and the sky, cerulean blue.

The glare from golden grasses and cattails told me Aunt Betty's Pond was close. There, I'd been told by a naturalist earlier in the day, brook trout, banded killifish, and sticklebacks live in the pond's marshy water, barely a yard deep.

Around the bend, Aunt Betty's Pond appeared like a table set with lily pads. This is a park to grow old in, I thought. ✦

About This Story

Terry Tempest Williams is an American writer, most closely associated with Utah's red rock desert. But as we learned in her book, *The Hour of Land,* her family has roots in Maine.

Williams defines the concept of the "ecotone" as where two ecologies meet, such as when forest meets ocean, or meadow meets woods—a tension which wooed us the first time we visited Acadia. But the ecotone also describes the "from here" (native-born, lifetime Mainers) and "from away" (non-Mainers) tension that has defined the cultural ecology in Acadia. Maybe because we're "from away" as well, it's Williams's writing that has come closest to capturing our loving, but temporary, experience of the park.

Acadia is where we built our love of the outdoors. It is a place that is as deeply meaningful for us, and for countless others, as it is for Williams, and hearing of her special connection only strengthens ours. This landscape has entered our DNA, an experience we expect you've had as well.

The Ballad of the Night
Charley Tended Weir

RUTH MOORE

Charley had a herring-weir
Down to Bailey's Bight;
Got up to tend it, in
The middle of the night,

Late October
Midnight black as tar;
Nothin' out the window but
A big cold star;

House like a cemetery;
Kitchen fire dead.
"I'm damn good mind," said Charley,
"To go back to bed.

"A man who runs a herring-weir,
Even on the side,
Is nothing but a slave to
The God damned tide."

Well, a man feels meager,
A man feels old,
In pitch-black midnight,
Lonesome and cold,

Chills in his stomach like
Forty thousand mice,
And the very buttons on his pants,
Little lumps of ice.

Times he gets to feeling
It's no damn use;
So Charley had a pitcherful
In his orange juice.

Then he felt better
Than he had before;
So he had another pitcherful
To last him to the shore.

Down by the beach-rocks,
Underneath a tree,
Charley saw something
He never thought he'd see;

Sparkling in the lantern light
As he went to pass,
Three big diamonds
In the frosty grass.

"H'm," he said. "Di'monds.
Where'd *they* come from?
I'll pick them up later on,
Always wanted some."

Then he hauled in his dory —
She felt light as air —
And in the dark midnight
Rowed off to tend weir.

Out by the weir-gate,
Charley found
An old sea serpent
Swimming round and round.

Head like a washtub;
Whiskers like thatch;
Breath like the flame on
A Portland Star match.

Black in the lantern light,
Up he rose,
A great big barnacle
On the end of his nose;

Looked Charley over,
Surly and cross.
"Them fish you got shut up in there,
Belongs to my boss."

"Fish?" says Charley.
"Fish? In there?
Why, I ain't caught a fish
Since I built that damn weir."

"Well," says the serpent,
"Nevertheless,
There's ten thousand bushels
At a rough guess."

Charley moved the lantern,
Gave his oars a pull,
And he saw that the weir was
Brim-belay full.

Fish rising out of water
A trillion at a time,
And the side of each and every one
Was like a silver dime.

"Well," says the sea serpent,
"What you going to do?
They're uncomfortable,
And they don't belong to you;

"So, open this contraption
Up and let 'em go.
Come on. Shake the lead out.
The boss says so."

"Does?" says Charley.
"Who in hell is he,
Thinks he can sit back
And send word to me?"

Sea serpent swivelled round,
Made a waterspout.
"Keep on, brother,
And you'll find out."

"Why," Charley says, "You're nothing
But a lie so old you're hoary;
So take your dirty whiskers
Off the gunnel of my dory!"

Sea serpent twizzled,
Heaved underneath,
Skun back a set of
Sharp yellow teeth,

Came at Charley
With a gurgly roar,
And Charley let him have it
With the port-side oar,

Right on the noggin;
Hell of a knock,
And the old sea serpent
Sank like a rock.

"So go on back," yells Charley,
"And tell the old jerk,
Not to send a boy
To do a man's work."

Then over by the weir-gate,
Tinkly and clear.
A pretty little voice says,
"Yoo-hoo, Charley, dear!"

"Now what?" says Charley.
"This ain't funny."
And the same sweet voice says,
"Yoo-hoo, Charley, honey."

And there on the seine-pole
Right in the weir,
Was a little green mermaid,
Combing out her hair.

"All right," says Charley.
"I see you.
And I know who you come from.
So you git, too!"

He let fly his bailing-scoop,
It landed with a *clunk*,
And when the water settled,
The mermaid, *she* had sunk.

Then the ocean moved behind him,
With a mighty heave and hiss,
And a thundery, rumbly voice remarked,
"I'm Goddamn sick of this!"

And up come an old man,
White from top to toe,
Whiter than a daisy field,
Whiter than the snow;

Carrying a pitchfork
With three tines on it,
Muttering in his whiskers,
And madder than a hornet.

"My sea serpent is so lame
That he can hardly stir,
And my best mermaid,
You've raised a lump on her;

"And you've been pretty sarsy
Calling me a jerk;
So, now the Old Man has come
To do a man's work."

"Look," says Charley,
"Why don't you leave me be?
You may be the hoary Old
Man of the sea,

"But, I've got a run of fish here,
Shut up inside,
And if you keep on frigging round
You'll make me lose the tide."

Then the next thing that Charley knew
He was lying on the sand;
The painter of his dory
Was right beside his hand.

He could see across the bay,
Calm and still and wide;
It was full daylight;
And it was high tide.

"H'm," says Charley.
"What am I about?"
The oars weren't wet, so
He hadn't been out.

"Oh," he thought. "Di'monds,
Underneath the tree.
Seems to me I found some.
I better go see."

But he couldn't find any;
Not one gem;
Only three little owl-dungs
With frost on them. ✦

About This Story

Behind the counter at Mount Desert Island's Southwest Harbor Public Library hangs a bumper sticker that says, "I READ RUTH MOORE."

Reading Ruth Moore is a badge of honor around these parts. The *New York Times* hailed Moore as "New England's only answer to Faulkner." She built her own house in Bass Harbor, and lived with her "friend," Eleanor Mayo, during a time when it was inappropriate for a woman to do such things. Moore chose to write well about life around her, because "Maine," she said, "is a microcosm of everywhere else."

This ballad captures the life of the New Englander, and was the very first story we discovered for this anthology. The evocative text and the singsongy language jumped out as exactly the type of campfire story we were looking for.

The Coming of Glooskap

Glooskap, The Man From Nothing, first called
the minds of his Red Children to his coming into the world
when the world contained no other man, in flesh, but himself.
When he opened his eyes lying on his back in the dust,
his head toward the rising of the sun,
and his feet toward the setting of the sun;
the right hand pointing to the north
and his left hand to the south.
Having no strength to move any part of his body,
yet the brightness of the day revealed to him
all the glories of the whole world:
the sun was at its highest standing still,
and beside it was the moon without motion
and the stars were in their fixed places
while the firmament was in its beautiful blue.
While yet his eyes were held fast in their sockets
he saw all that the world contained.
Beside what the region of the air revealed to him,
he saw the land, the sea:
mountains, lakes, rivers, and the motion of the waters;
and in it he saw the fishes.
On the land were the animals and beasts,
and in the air the birds.

In the direction of the rising sun
he saw the night approaching.

While the body clung to the dust
he was without mind,
and the flesh without feeling.
At that moment the heavens were lit up,
with all kinds of bright colors most beautiful,
each color stood by itself,
and in another moment
every color shot a streak into the other,
and soon all the colors intermingled,
forming a beautiful brightness in the center of the heavens
over the front of his face.
Nearer and nearer came the brightness toward his body
until it got almost to a touching distance,
and a feeling came into his flesh,
he felt the warmth of the approaching brightness,
and he fell into a deep sleep.

The wind of the heavens fanned his brow,
and the sense of seeing returned to him,
but he saw not the brightness he beheld before,
but instead of the brightness
a person like unto himself,
standing at his right hand,
and the person's face was toward the rising of the sun.
In silence he raised his right hand
in the direction of the rising sun,
passed it from thence to the setting of the sun,
and immediately a streak of lightning
followed the motion of his hand
from one side of the earth to the other.

Again he raised his right hand to the south,
passing it to the north,
and immediately another streak of lightning
followed the motion of his hand.
Immediately after the passing of the lightning over his body
a sense of thought came into him,
and the Great Spirit answered his thought
saying these words:

"Arise from thy bed of dust
and stand on thy feet,
let the dust be under thy feet,
and as thou believest,
thou shall have strength to walk."

Immediately strength came into him,
and he arose to his feet,
and stood beside the Great Spirit. ✦

About This Story

Joseph Nicolar was an elder and political leader of the Penobscot Nation of Maine, one of the five tribes that make up the Wabanaki Confederacy. He served six terms as the tribe's elected representative to the Maine State Legislature. Witnessing a growing threat to his culture, Nicolar self-published *The Life and Traditions of the Red Man* in 1893 to preserve the Penobscot cultural heritage for future generations of the tribe.

In this profoundly beautiful legend, Nicolar tells of the coming of Glooskap. Glooskap is the Creator, and hero, of many Wabanaki stories. As is shown in this legend, Glooskap is "the man who came from nothing." There are many variations on this Glooskap legend because, for American Indians, storytelling is a living form that can change from storyteller to storyteller, and even each time a story is told. But most stories about Glooskap represent him as kind, benevolent, and engaged in a fight against evil powers. Glooskap is such an important figure that a story about his coming is, in turn, a story about the beginning of the world.

Excerpt from
We Were an Island

Arrival & First Two Days, June 8–9, 1949

PETER P. BLANCHARD III

here they were, husband and wife, both thirty-eight years of age and high up on the shingle beach of their new found land. Having been ferried ashore with their belongings and supplies, Art and Nan Kellam entered a shared state of amazement and gratitude as they surveyed Placentia for the first time as island owners. The 552-acre island lay before them, resplendent in the Gulf of Maine, two miles out to sea. The Kellams had voyaged out to Placentia in a brand new wooden dory, towed by Cliff Rich, the dory's builder. After relaying his good wishes to the couple at the very edge of their adventure, Cliff turned his workboat toward McKinley on Mt. Desert Island. As Cliff's skiff receded from view, the din of his outboard engine gave way to more subtle and natural sounds. These sounds had prevailed along the Maine coast since prehistoric time—the rush and clatter of beach stones as waves advanced and retreated and the strident cries of gulls, wheeling over the Bar at the island's northeastern tip.

From their vantage point, the newcomers could actually see only a small portion of their kingdom. Nevertheless, they already had a good sense of its entirety. Great ledges of pink granite led off to the south of their position and a shingle beach stretched to the north, linking with the Bar. Behind the couple lay the great wall of an evergreen forest. In contrast, their view to the east was very much unimpeded. Across an expanse of water three quarters of a mile wide, Art and Nan could see their immediate island neighbor—Great Gott or Gotts Island, which was barred to Little Gotts Island to the south. To the southeast lay the other member of their small archipelago (or group of islands)—Black Island, apparently so named because of the thickness of its spruce cover. Nestled in the center of Great Gott's western shore was the only year-round community in the island group, evidenced by a small cluster of buildings that had changed little since the nineteenth century. In recent memory, the remaining islands had been inhabited, if at all, by summer residents. For two former inlanders, transplanted from California's canyon lands, the maritime world that now extended before them was a new and entrancing reality.

The couple's novel acquisition had a curious name, "Placentia." That name probably dated back to the time of early French exploration along the Maine coast, during the seventeenth century. The translation of the earliest recorded name, "Plaisance," is "pleasure yachting or sailing." "Plaisance"—evidently inspired by the island's long, ship-like profile, as seen from the water—was either misinterpreted or mispronounced by later English settlers in the region. The result was the modern form, "Placentia." Local usage then transformed "Placentia" into "Plasench."

A remarkable transference of identity was soon made by local people who knew of the Kellams' endeavor. The island, the dory, and the couple began to receive the appellation of "Plasench" interchangeably. Watching the dory as it approached the wharf at McKinley or rode the swells of the sea passage, Mainers could readily be heard to say, "Here comes Plasench!" or "There goes Plasench!" The same expression was applied to Art and Nan when, quite removed from the dory and the island, they were seen navigating on dry land on Mt. Desert. Thus, for example, observant customers would have taken note as "Plasench" passed along the aisles of Reed's General Store in McKinley or pondered purchases at Sawyer's Market in Southwest Harbor.

With little or no nautical experience in their past, Art and Nan Kellam felt that taking on island ownership and residence was like taking over the helm of a great ship. One playful and joyful thought was that this vessel would never need an anchor or running lights. And she would have right of way over all other vessels at sea! The comparison of spruce-clad Placentia with a sailing schooner or tall ship was provided by Nan in the following passage, which evoked the magic of the morning on June 9, 1949, their first full day on the island.

Only a few feet away, a barely roughened sea lay pink to the sunrise as I wakened. . . . From a sleeping bag, stretched on a slope of shingle beach, I watched dawn's changing colors heightened on a tranquil, unfamiliar scene. Art stood in the foreground beside a driftwood fire, bending a length of iron rod into a homemade grate. To his left, stem to the water, lay a shining new dory anchored just above the wrack line that marked high tide; beyond on the bank loomed a broad pile of dunnage, stacked off-stage like props of a waiting set.

All of the elements of the surroundings, though strange in themselves, merged easily to a sense of something pleasant dreamed again. June 9, 1949 had dawned at last, and an ocean island had become our home.

While I dressed in stiff new overalls and climbed among the loose beach stones, gathering more wood for a breakfast fire, small unaccustomed smoke clouds puffed off from Placentia's shore. Above them, gray gulls took turns of survey, diving now and then, to question in loud harsh voices our right to their established claim. In the air everywhere hung a lively fragrance, the soft smell of forest and the sharp tang of sea combined closely, harmoniously, like notes of a major chord.

In the midst of this different world, Art worked away, patient as always with a project. Before long, his odd piece of handiwork rested on rock pillars over the glowing coals. Only the first of a long line of island improvisations, the grate would last through many months and meals—in fact, till Old Ocean, shifting the beach in a strong southeaster, buried it beyond recall.

On this quiet morning, bacon browned over the grill, while we ate on the rocks, watching two lobster boats working offshore. The fisherman made a slow, irregular course, hauling in here, casting back there, now and again directing toward Plasench a ship-to-shore glance, frankly curious.

As well it might be. The ponderous pile on the bank must have looked like the birth of a colony or the means of abandoning civilization forever. Actually, for beginners, it was a conservative collection. Our modest tangle of goods matched a wish to leave behind the battle for non-essentials and the burden of abundance—and to build in the beauty of this million-masted island a simple home and an uncluttered life.

Of course, so grand a goal must be far ahead. But preliminaries had ended. Time had come now to sort out our own most urgent needs. They could easily be narrowed down to three: fresh water; a shelter above our heads and a weatherproof place to store supplies.

Art and Nan chose a natural cover for their first two nights on Placentia. During their one reconnaissance mission to the island in the spring of 1948, Berl Gott, a lobsterman and guide, had shown the couple the remnants of several aging structures—a tottering barn and a small wooden shed—on the wooded hillside, well inland from their landing beach. During their first days in residence on the island in June 1949, Art and Nan regarded this site as their base of operations and began to haul belongings up to the barn. Nevertheless, the Kellams were determined to sleep, at least for the first few nights, under a magnificent white spruce that dominated the northeastern shore. Well over one hundred years ago, this giant appeared to have stepped forward from the line of the forest to take a solitary position at the crest of the beach, nearer the water's edge.

Art and Nan spent the night of June 8 in their sleeping bags, side by side, under the boughs of the great evergreen, which they named the "Lonesome Spruce." This tree was to become a physical and an emotive landmark—a rallying point of their island days. There was a gentle breeze from the south, and the constellations, with which they would soon become very familiar, intensified in the darkening sky. Most probably, sleep for Placentia's two new denizens came quickly. The feel of the flat, shifting beach stones under their bedding, the novel sounds of the advancing and retreating tide within feet of their resting place, and the excitement at spending the night on their very own island were probably countered by exhaustion. Their writings are a bit mysterious about that first night, other than noting its serenity.

Given the significance of those first days on island—days in which Art and Nan had to take bearings and literally establish a foothold—a review of the corresponding Journal entries is illuminating. The following two entries from the Journal provide an introduction to the Kellams' idiosyncratic vocabulary—a special avenue of communication that existed between husband and wife. Examples from the extracts below include "BLB" (Bear loves Beum, the name of their wooden dory), "Bear" (Art), and "Bears" (Art and Nan). As was her custom, Nan made the following journal entries in pencil and in graceful script:

[June 8, 1949]

Wednesday about 3 p.m. arrived on Placentia Island in the BLB, purchased June 7th from Mr. Clifton Rich, its builder, in Bernard, Me.

With some help from Mr. Rich, deposited part of our gear in shack, waved farewell to our tow and began island life on our own. Long exploration tour thru the woods. Bear worried about the tide vs. the BLB, and hurried on to rescue it. When Beum [Nan] rounded the bar corner, there was a bear Bear shaking hands with himself gaily. He had been swimming in the ocean, making the boat safe. Full moon. Best dinner ever—driftwood fire. Two happy bears settled to sleep on the beach—at home at last!

[June 9, 1949]

With intent to start working hard, we arose to the clamor of the sea gulls on the bar at sunup, cooked breakfast, and made for new headquarters, the shepherd's shack, ½ mi. above dory mooring. Located in a daisy meadow, surrounded by spruce and fir. Mr. R [Rich] pointed out an old apple orchard, which perhaps we can salvage. Built a ladder; re-shingled part of Lil' Homewood [the Kellams' first island shelter]; tacked a strip of gay awning material . . . over the roof's ridge. Investigated old sheep barn, finding plenty of good boards for a new shack floor, shelves, etc. Another nite on our excellent pebbled beach; moonlight on dark, densely-wooded Black Island and meager settlement on Little Gott. Able to see Bass Harbor Light better then expected and hope to find a beach for landing there. What wealth could one exchange for these beautiful days and nites and our glorious freedom! Like prolonged vacation, and Art is my darling—enthusiastic and very sunburned. ✦

About This Story

Stop me if you've had this thought while on vacation—"What if I didn't go back? What if I lived here instead?" This excerpt from Peter P. Blanchard's book, *We Were an Island*, follows Art and Nan Kellam on their first day of doing just that: rowing out to the island they've just purchased and sleeping right under the stars. The Kellams would live together on Placentia Island year-round for the next forty years.

We learned about Art and Nan around a campfire after a show at Barn Arts Collective, a theater group on the Mount Desert Island's quiet side. Barn Arts had been sifting through Nan's journals at the Southwest Harbor Library, and were just as enthralled as we were by these hermits off the Maine coast.

Reading Nan's journals and Blanchard's account of their experience help you to see that the Kellams' story is a story of love. That Art and Nan, who called each other "Bear" and "Beum," chose to live on the rugged coast of Maine's shore because they decided that all they would ever need was one another. It's this foundation of love that makes the Kellams' story so compelling, and so endearing.

Koluskap naka Pukcinsqehs: of Koluskap and the Witch that loved him.

AS TOLD BY GEO NEPTUNE

When the world was created, the Creator knew there was still much work to be done, so they created Koluskap. Koluskap was gifted with strong spiritual powers to help him complete this work. In addition to the plants, animals, and people on the earth, there were also monsters, giants, and other creatures of darkness that inhabited the Dawnland. One of these dark creatures was Pukcinsqehs, a witch. Pukcinsqehs, whose name is also that for a small bottle, jug, or pitcher, was a very powerful and very dark sorceress. While she had multiple talents, her most famous power was her ability to change from woman to man. But one of her deepest desires was to become a mother, and she tried many times to have her own child, and gave birth to many gruesome monsters in the process. She so desperately wanted a beautiful child that she often stole Wabanaki children and attempted to raise them as her own.

Pukcinsqehs eventually fell in love with Koluskap, thinking that together they could rule the Dawnland with their incredible powers. Koluskap did not return her love, however, and she quickly became filled with rage. She vowed to exact revenge upon Koluskap, and did everything she could to make Koluskap's work more difficult. She also began to direct her rage towards Koluskap's children, the Wabanaki. For many years she tormented Koluskap, eventually kidnapping his family members, Grandmother Woodchuck and Nephew Marten.

A long chase ensued over many seasons, with Koluskap always close behind Pukcinsqehs and his grandmother and nephew. Eventually he caught up to the witch, and approached her camp undetected. When his Nephew Marten was ordered to collect firewood away from camp, Koluskap surprised him, and disclosed his plan for rescuing Marten and Grandmother Woodchuck. One of Marten's responsibilities was to care for Pukcinsqehs' most recent child, and Koluskap told Marten that when he was ordered by Pukcinsqehs to fetch the babe, he should throw it into the fireplace and call out to Koluskap.

When the moment came to pass that Marten was ordered to fetch the babe of Pukcinsqehs, he followed Koluskap's instructions carefully. As he carried the infant past the fire, he tossed it into the fireplace and immediately fled for the safety of Koluskap. He ran, calling out to his uncle, with the wrathful Pukcinsqehs close behind him. Using his power, Koluskap grew himself to a mighty size and stepped out to surprise Pukcinsqehs. As Koluskap had foreseen, Pukcinsqehs was too distracted by her anger to use her own powers, and fled. There followed an epic chase through the Dawnland.

As she ran, Pukcinsqehs began to regain control of her emotions, and willed herself to grow with each step. Koluskap and Pukcinsqehs each grew to such size that their footsteps sounded like thunder, and their snowshoes left imprints in the earth and rocks throughout the Dawnland. Eventually, Koluskap caught up to Pukcinsqehs on the island of Pesamkuk. In the middle of a range of mountains, Pemotonet, Koluskap caught Pukcinsqehs by her hair and threw her to the ground.

As Koluskap held her by the hair, Pukcinsqehs began to laugh, only further maddening Koluskap. Growing himself to his largest size, he began to stomp Pukcinsqehs into the ground. As he stomped, Pukcinsqehs laughed louder and louder, only adding to his rage. When Koluskap finally calmed himself enough to remove his foot, he looked down in horror at what he had done. By stomping on the witch, he had helped her change from a singular being into millions of tiny, biting insects: the first mosquitoes and black flies. As she swarmed around Koluskap and away from the island of Pesamkuk, she said to the giant, "Thank you for your help, Koluskap. Now I may torment your children forever." ✦

About This Story

From the moment we met Geo Neptune, a member of the Passamaquoddy tribe, he was overflowing with stories. Having grown up in Indian Township, Maine, Geo now serves as an educator, basket maker, and storyteller at Abbe Museum. The next time you're in downtown Bar Harbor, check out this museum to learn more about the Wabanaki.

The Wabanaki (translated roughly as "People of the Dawnland") are an American Indian confederation composed of five principal nations: the Mi'kmaq, Maliseet, Passamaquoddy, Abenaki, and Penobscot. They are the native people of Acadia and can celebrate being one of the rare exceptions: the creation of a national park did not result in the expulsion of the tribe. The Wabanaki have always been, and continue to be, on Mount Desert Island.

Geo was excited to share this story about Koluskap, the hero of many Wabanaki stories. The events of this story occur right on Mount Desert Island, and explain why black flies and mosquitoes swarm the island in early spring. We couldn't have asked for a more generous guide to the Wabanaki culture, and are thrilled to share his telling of this classic story.

The Burning Tree

ELMER BEAL JR.

The summer has gone, and the day's growing cold
Far away honk some geese in their flight
Here down below, we start thinking of snow
And the quiet of long winter nights
But even though times may get harder
And the darkness can make you feel old
There's a good harvest stored in the larder
And the trees are aflame now, in red, green, and gold

Too many times when I'm driving, I'm blind
Swept along thinking I've got to be
First in the line, 'till my teeth start to grind
Like the cobblestones down by the sea
But yesterday morning at sunrise
where the highway dips down by the sea
The fire of dawn was reflected
In the leaves of a tree that was beckoning to me

And I run through the leaves in the cool autumn breeze
Feeling warmed by the fire in me
Though it's said they don't talk, I still learn a lot
In the light of the burning trees

There on the ground, I heard a voice with no sound
Saying "this is your reason to be"
To seek your own place in this whole human race
And to find it will set your heart free
But even though times will get harder
And the darkness will make you feel old
There's a good harvest stored in the larder
And the wisdom you hear in the trees is your soul ✦

About This Story

The son of a lobsterman and folk singer, Elmer Beal Jr.'s award-winning restaurant, The Burning Tree, takes its name from one of his folk songs.

The crisp, cool nights and bright, sunny days of fall in New England create its intoxicating red, green, and gold foliage. The thousands of tourists who pour into New England during this season are affectionately known as "leaf peepers." We began this crazy *Campfire Stories* trip here, swept away by the search for stories, and searching for our place in the world. But, much like Elmer in this song, we found moments where the brilliant fall backdrop took our breath away, and where the wisdom of the burning trees served as our guide.

Fire

WILLIAM CARPENTER

This morning, on the opposite shore of the river,
I watch a man burning his own house.
It is a cold day, and the man wears thick gloves
and a fur hat that gives him a Russian look.
I envy his energy, since I'm still on the sunporch
in my robe, with morning coffee, my day not
even begun, while my neighbor has already piled
spruce boughs against his house and poured
flammable liquids over them to send a ribbon
of black smoke into the air, a column surrounded
by herring gulls, who think he's having a barbecue
or has founded a new dump. I hadn't known what labor
it took to burn something. Now the man's working
at such speed, he's like the criminal in a silent
movie, as if he had a deadline, as if he had
to get his house burned by a certain time, or it
would be all over. I see his kids helping, bringing
him matches and kindling, and I'd like to help out
myself, I'd like to bring him coffee and a bagel,
but the Penobscot River separates us, icebergs
the size of small ships drifting down the tide.
Moreover, why should I help him when I have a house
myself, which needs burning as much as anyone's?

It has begun to leak. I think it has carpenter ants.
I hear them making sounds at night like writing, only
they aren't writing, they are building small tubular
cities inside the walls. I start burning in the study,
working from within so it will go faster, so I can
catch up, and soon there's a smoke column on either
side, like a couple of Algonquins having a dialogue
on how much harder it is to destroy than to create.
I shovel books and poems into the growing fire. If
I burn everything, I can start over, with a future
like a white rectangle of paper. Then I notice
my neighbor has a hose, that he's spraying his house
with water, the coward, he has bailed out, but I
keep throwing things into the fire: my stamps,
my Berlioz collection, my photos of nude people,
my correspondence dating back to grade school.
Over there, the fire engines are reaching his home.
His wife is crying with relief, his fire's extinguished.
He has walked down to the shore to see the ruins
of the house across the river, the open cellar,
the charred timbers, the man laughing and singing
in the snow, who has been finally freed from his
possessions, who has no clothes, no library, who has
gone back to the beginning, when we lived in nature:
no refuge from the elements, no fixed address. ✦

About This Story

Bill Carpenter was one of the first people we spoke with when we began our journey to understand Acadia. Bill is a full-time faculty of literature and writing at the College of the Atlantic, and the only remaining faculty from the founding of the college in 1969. He enthusiastically recounted how the College of the Atlantic was formed on Mount Desert Island, a unique biological setting with a national park as an extended campus.

It was a pleasant surprise to come across Carpenter's writing in *Maine Speaks: An Anthology of Maine Literature*. His poem captures so much of the Maine experience. With countless coastal islands and inland lakes and tributaries, it's common to find oneself across a river from the nearest neighbor. His decision to burn his own house to simplify his life is classic Maine humor—dry as a bone with a touch of darkness, but making perfect sense in its own rugged way.

GREAT SMOKY MOUNTAINS NATIONAL PARK

Home in the Mountains of Blue Smoke

NESTLED ON THE BORDER of North Carolina and Tennessee, Great Smoky Mountains is the most visited national park in the country. It offers stunning views of the oldest mountain range on the planet, scenic drives slowed by "bear jams," and a rich human history.

illustration by
SARAH JACOBY

A s we drove to the Great Smoky Mountains, it seemed appropriate to listen to *The National Parks: America's Best Idea*, by Dayton Duncan and Ken Burns, on tape. We were struck by an interview with Gerard Baker, the first American Indian superintendent of the national parks, where he said, "When you walk into any natural, national park, you are walking into someone's homeland."

This is doubly true for Great Smoky Mountains National Park. Spanning both North Carolina and Tennessee, these gentle mountains were once home to hundreds of families, American Indian and European alike. When the park was formed in 1934, it spurred the relocation of hundreds of these families. Some accepted the government's offers for their land, but others fought to remain, resulting in a complex history that lingers today.

The park's preservation saved much of the forest from further logging, and nearby towns Gatlinburg and Pigeon Forge experienced significant growth as a result of the new tourism industry. These communities, who raised part of the funds to purchase the land, see the value of the park and its ongoing preservation. And, to their credit, the National Park Service supported lifetime leases for a few mountain families (like the famous Walker Sisters), and hired Joseph Hall (a.k.a. "the Song Catcher") to collect recordings of mountain culture. The Park Service sought to preserve the Appalachian culture it was disbanding. Today, the Great Smoky Mountains are rich with stories of the Appalachian way of life.

Those who trace their ancestors to these mountains have kept their spiritual connection to the land. They revere the wisdom of the smoke, the gentle curves of the old mountains, and the call to a simple and rich way of life. Everyday mountain life was rugged, and people used a variety of ingenious methods to live off the land. Without higher education, or access to doctors, mountain communities relied on home remedies and superstitions to guide their daily decisions. Lice was treated with kerosene, and moon phases guided when and where to plant or harvest crops. Despite Prohibition, turning corn into moonshine (a.k.a. corn liquor) was so profitable that many farmers owned and operated illegal stills.

But the story of European settlers in the Appalachians is just one side of this region's history. Archaeological digs show that the Cherokee have lived in the Smokies for tens of thousands of years. Yet, one hundred years before the park was established, they were driven out when President Andrew Jackson signed the Indian Removal Act. It called for all American Indians east of the Mississippi to be relocated to "Indian territory": present-day Oklahoma. Some members of the Eastern Band of Cherokee Indians were able to remain, either through land ownership claims or by refusing to relocate, and would go on to establish the Qualla Boundary, a sovereign nation within North Carolina. Today, the Cherokee govern themselves in the Qualla Boundary, where they continue to teach their language and culture, with ongoing festivals, craft markets, trout fishing tournaments, and the annual Miss Cherokee competition. Storytelling is also a large part of how the Cherokee pass down important values and lessons to the next generation, even as every story varies slightly each time it's told.

We were welcomed to the Great Smoky Mountains in early May by a week of heavy, cold rain, dampening our enthusiasm at kicking off the second leg of our trip. One evening, after a dinner of soggy beans at our campsite, the voice of an earnest singer, backed by a standup bass and banjo, drifted towards us. Like a siren in the sea, the sound lured us. Under the awning of a camping trailer sat friends and family watching a rotating cast of performers. When we arrived, three elderly women were crooning an old hymn with a three-piece band. We stood outside the awning, giddily smiling and clapping along, when one of the singers and her husband enthusiastically exclaimed, "You need to get in closer and hear 'em sing! They do this every year. Everybody's friends here—there's no strangers. Get a little closer, you'll really enjoy it!" Soaked, and half the age of the youngest person there, we were grateful to be received with such warmth from strangers who offered us blankets, chairs, and a good view. Appalachian mountain music is a genre of folk music that precedes bluegrass, and is played acoustically with an assortment of stringed instruments—fiddles, mandolins, guitars, and banjos—that could be made at home. For gatherings without instruments, there is shape-note singing, a sheet music system that uses shapes to help everyone find the note. The resourcefulness of mountain people has colored the traditions of Appalachian music.

With rain also comes fog. The Smokies get their name from the fog over the mountains, typically occurring in the mornings or after rainfall. We've heard of many origins for the smoke: that it's humid air from the Gulf of Mexico cooling rapidly in this climate, that it's moisture from the trees, or that it's the prayers of all the Cherokee people making their way up to the gods. No matter which you believe, the smoke that hangs over the mountains gives this emerald palace an aura of wisdom. The Appalachian mountain range is one of the oldest on the planet, thought to once have been as tall as the Rocky Mountains before being worn down by weather, time, and the constant shifting of the earth. The majority of the sand that today can be found along the coastlines of the Atlantic Ocean is made up of the very particles that once formed the highest peaks of the Appalachian Mountains. Today, these wise old mountains appear "gentle," like "grandmother's bosom," as some locals say, but they can be deceptively difficult to explore.

That first week of rain gave way to blooming tulip poplars (among many other wildflowers) and two weeks of allergies. The Smokies are referred to as the "womb of the earth," home to over 19,000 unique species of flora and fauna. No glacier covered any of the Appalachian mountains during the most recent ice age, due to the mountains' southwest-northeast angle. As the ice age ended, the species in the Smokies were able to fan out and repopulate North America. Today, the climate at the highest elevations of the mountains is suitable for a variety of New England species, while the valleys' climate is comfortable for species most at home in Georgia or Alabama. There are more plant classes here than anywhere else in North America.

And then there are the "bear jams." An unexpected part of our journey were the frequent traffic jams caused by possible bear sightings. There are 1,600 black bears and 11 million visitors in the park each year, and neither behave responsibly. During our stay, a backcountry camper on the Appalachian Trail was bitten in the leg by a bear, through his tent. A few days later, the bear wandered back into the campsite, and had to be euthanized. Once a bear sees humans as a source of food, everyone is in danger. An ongoing challenge for park officials is to keep people safe, and keep wild animals wild.

While many think of black bears when they think of the Great Smoky Mountains, it is also considered the Salamander Capital of the World. On average, there's one black bear for every square mile of park, but if you took all the salamanders in just one square mile, they would outweigh not just the bears, but every other species in that square mile combined. While most visitors don't come to see the salamanders, many do visit in June to catch a glimpse of the thousands of fireflies lighting up the night in unison.

Fascinated by the flora and fauna of the region, we signed ourselves up for a daylong hike with the Friends of the Smokies to Hyatt Ridge. It was going to be a slow but long ascent and, so early into the trip, we were nervous about our stamina, but when we looked at the other dozen hikers, all middle-aged or older, we breathed a sigh of relief. Left foot, right foot, left foot, right foot, up, up, and up ... within two hours of the ten-hour hike, Ilyssa had already pulled off to the side of the trail a handful of times, and we were at the rear of the group. We thought her fatigue must be due to her asthma, or the unusually high spring pollen count— the kind that leaves behind a yellow coating on car windows. Or, surely, the moonshine we had days ago couldn't still be keeping us down ... could it? After several attempts to catch up with the group, we had to admit defeat, and ask to be escorted down the mountain by the kind park ranger who had volunteered to support the hike. Hours later, after a nap at the campsite, we wondered what had happened to us. Did the pollen take its toll? Were we not cut out for four months of living out of a tent? And, later, can cold, wet weather and poor sleep delay ... a period?

The answer is no. But being pregnant can.

Prelude

JAMES WILLIS HEMBREE

To attune the ear to music,
  Just a few notes to suffice,
If a treasure you are seeking,
Let Ol' Smoky be the prize.

Down where dear ol' North Carolina
Grasps the hand of Tennessee,
There the mighty Smoky Mountains
Rise with joyous ecstasy.

'Tis a land that's filled with beauty,
Overflowing with good cheer,
That's just why a tourist shouted
To his driver, "Let's park here."

Many days they roamed the mountains,
What a treasure did they find!
In that wonderland of beauty—
Sweet contentment for the mind.

There they found the wealth of sunshine,
And the friendship of the trees,
Heard the ripple of the waters,
Found the fragrance of the breeze.

To the ear in tune for music
Nature sang a wondrous song,
All the birds joined in the chorus,
Sweetly singing all day long.

There the tall grass seemed to whisper
Satisfaction to the soul,
With the sweetest flowers blooming,
Joy was theirs to have an' hold.

When, at last, the rambles ended,
And the tourists went away,
Telling stories of the mountains,
Folks kept coming ever' day.

While the peaks of grand "Ol' Smoky"
Rising up to kiss the blue,
Kindo' told the folks, in silence,
What they really ought to do.

Then ol' Tennessee got busy,
North Carolina lent a hand,
And they, both worked hard together,
Raising money for the land,

Tho' it seemed the dream would vanish,
Of a park the folks would doubt,
'Till the mighty Rockefeller
Gave a fund to help them out.

You can sing' your Hallelujahs!
Let them ring from morn' 'til dark,
For the land our Nation's taken
As the "Smoky Mountains Park." ✦

About This Story

Depending on who you ask about the founding of Great Smoky Mountains National Park, you're likely to hear a different story. Each version starts with the desire to create a national park, despite the challenge of relocating the many mountain families that inhabited these lands. A historian might tell you that North Carolina and Tennessee negotiated 6,000 separate land leases. Locals may recall manning phone banks to raise the money to purchase the land: even schoolchildren donated their piggy banks to help preserve this place. And one tour guide we met told us that five or six mountain families donated land to the government on the condition that the park would always be fee-free.

Storytellers told us to "never let the truth ruin a good story." Historians, on the other hand, said "a story is worth nothing if it isn't true." With both of these pieces of advice in mind, we present Hembree's song, which captures the music and wisdom of these mountains for the storytellers, while providing an account of the park's founding that historians can also get behind.

Excerpt from
A Walk in the Woods

BILL BRYSON

Once, aeons ago, the Appalachians were of a scale and majesty to rival the Himalayas—piercing, snow-peaked, pushing breathtakingly through the clouds to heights of four miles or more. New Hampshire's Mount Washington is still an imposing presence, but the stony mass that rises from the New England woods today represents, at most, the stubby bottom one-third of what was ten million years ago.

That the Appalachian Mountains present so much more modest an aspect today is because they have had so much time in which to wear away. The Appalachians are immensely old—older than the oceans and continents (at least in their present configurations), far, far older than most other mountain chains, older indeed than almost all other landscape features on earth. When simple plants colonized the land and the first creatures crawled gasping from the sea, the Appalachians were there to greet them.

Something over a billion years ago, the continents of earth were a single mass called Pangaea surrounded by the lonely Panthalassan Sea. Then some unexplained turmoil within the earth's mantle caused the land to break apart and drift off as vast asymmetrical chunks. From time to time over the ages since—three times at least—the continents have held a kind of grand reunion, floating back to some central spot and bumping together with slow but crushing force. It was during the third of these collisions, starting about 470 million years ago, that the Appalachians were first pushed up (like a rucked carpet, as the analogy nearly always has it). Four hundred seventy million years is a span pretty well beyond grasping, but if you can imagine flying backwards through time at the rate of one year per second, it would take you about sixteen years to cover such a period. It's a long time.

The continents didn't just move in and out from each other in some kind of grand slow-motion square dance but spun in lazy circles, changed their orientation, went on cruises to the tropics and poles, made friends with smaller landmasses and brought them home. Florida once belonged to Africa. A corner of Staten Island is, geologically, part of Europe. The seaboard from New England up to Canada appears to have originated in Morocco. Parts of Greenland, Ireland, Scotland, and Scandinavia have the same rocks as the eastern United States—are, in effect, ruptured outposts of the Appalachians. There are even suggestions that mountains as far south as the Shackleton Range in Antarctica may be fragments of the Appalachian family.

The Appalachians were formed in three long phases (or orogenies, as geologists like to call them) known as the Taconic, Acadian, and Alleghenian. The first two were essentially responsible for the northern Appalachians, the third for the central and southern Appalachians. As the continents bumped and nudged, sometimes one continental plate would slide over another, pushing ocean floor before it, reworking the landscape for 150 miles or more inland. At other times it would plunge beneath, stirring up the mantle and resulting in long spells of volcanic activity and earthquakes. Sometimes the collisions would interleave layers of rock like shuffled playing cards.

It is tempting to think of this as some kind of giant continent-sized car crash, but of course it happened with imperceptible slowness. The proto-Atlantic Ocean (sometimes more romantically called Iapetus), which filled the void between continents during one of the early splits, looks in most textbook illustrations like a transitory puddle—there in Fig. 9A, vanished in Fig. 9B, as if the sun had come out for a day or so and dried it up—yet it existed far longer, hundreds of millions of years longer, than our own Atlantic has. So it was with the formation of mountains. If you were to travel back to one of the mountain-building phases of the Appalachians, you wouldn't be aware of anything geologically grand going on, any more than we are sensible now that India is plowing into Asia like a runaway truck into a snowbank, pushing the Himalayas up by a millimeter or so a year.

And as soon as the mountains were built, they began, just as ineluctably, to wear away. For all their seeming permanence, mountains are exceedingly transitory features. In *Meditations at 10,000 Feet*, writer and geologist James Trefil calculates that a typical mountain stream will carry away about 1,000 cubic feet of mountain in a year, mostly in the form of sand granules and other suspended particles. That is equivalent to the capacity of an average-sized dump truck—clearly not much at all. Imagine a dump truck arriving once each year at the base of a mountain, filling up with a single load, and driving off, not to reappear for another twelve months. At such a rate it seems impossible that it could ever cart away a mountain, but in fact given sufficient time that is precisely what would happen. Assuming a mountain 5,000 feet high with 500,000 million cubic feet of mass—roughly the size of Mount Washington—a single stream would level it in about 500 million years.

Of course most mountains have several streams and moreover are exposed to a vast range of other reductive factors, from the infinitesimal acidic secretions of lichen (tiny but relentless!) to the grinding scrape of ice sheets, so most mountains vanish very much more quickly—in a couple of hundred million years, say. Right now the Appalachians are shrinking on average by 0.03 millimeters per year. They have gone through this cycle at least twice, possibly more—rising to awesome heights, eroding away to nothingness, rising again, each time recycling their component materials in a dazzlingly confused and complex geology.

The detail of all this is theory, you understand. Very little of it is more than generally agreed upon. Some scientists believe the Appalachians experienced a fourth, earlier mountain-building episode, called the Grenville Orogeny, and that there may have been others earlier still. Likewise, Pangaea may have split and reformed not three times but a dozen times, or perhaps a score of times. On top of all this, there are a number of lapses in the theory, chief of which is that there is little direct evidence of continental collisions, which is odd, even inexplicable, if you accept that at least three continents rubbed together with enormous force for a period of at least 150 million years. There ought to be a suture, a layer of scar tissue, stretching up the eastern seaboard of the United States. There isn't. ✦

About This Story

Bill Bryson's *A Walk in the Woods* captures one man's quest to thru-hike the entire 2,190 miles of the Appalachian Trail. Stretching from Georgia to Maine, the Appalachian Trail has so much culture, legacy, and lore that it could fill its own volume of *Campfire Stories*. For this collection, we're focusing on where the trail runs through Great Smoky Mountains National Park, along the border of North Carolina and Tennessee.

Bryson is not a scientist, but that's what makes his contemplation on the Appalachian Mountains' geology so relatable. When we looked out from Clingmans Dome, we shared in his wonder at trying to comprehend the hundreds of millions of years of history of these rolling hills. Bryson shows us that it's the history of these mountains that makes hiking its paths profound.

The Birds and Animals Stickball Game

KATHI SMITH LITTLEJOHN

At one time,
many years ago,
human beings and animals
could talk the same language
It was a very magic time.
And more than that,
the animals and the birds
could talk the same language, too.
They all had good times together,
but occasionally they would argue.
Occasionally they would start to fight,
and sometimes they would even hurt one another.
One day the birds argued with the animals
that they were number one.
They were stronger, they were better, they were better looking.
They argued back and forth,
and finally it almost broke into a war.
So they decided that they would do what the Cherokee men did:
they would settle this by playing a game of stickball,
and they set up the game.
Animals and birds came from miles around to bet on the game.
They were real excited.

This was going to be the battle to end all the arguments
   who was going to be number one forever.
And the game started.
First the birds scored,
   and then the animals scored,
   then the birds would score,
   then the animals would score,
   and finally it was tied up.
Eleven-eleven.
Whoever would score the next point would win the game,
   because the games end at twelve.
The birds got the ball, and they were streaking toward the goal,
   and they dropped it.
Oh, no.
The animals got the ball,
   and they threw it from one to another,
   and they finally threw it to their secret weapon,
   Mr. Skunk.
Mr. Skunk put that ball in his mouth,
   and he started waddling down the field,
   and everybody backed off.
Nobody wanted to tackle Mr. Skunk.
"Go for it, go for it, get the ball, he's gonna score."
Finally Mr. Buzzard, brave Mr. Buzzard, swooped down.
He grabbed the skunk so hard
   he ripped a white streak right down his back
   that he still has today.
And skunk sprayed him.
Oh, shoo, did he spray him.
He sprayed him so bad, and he stunk so much
   that even today he flies all by himself,
  all alone,
   because he still stinks bad.

Oh, and Mr. Owl said,

"No, I can do it, I can do it."

And he swooped down and he tried to get the ball and he got
sprayed.

He got sprayed so bad it knocked rings around his eyes,
and he still has those today.

Finally Mr. Bluejay said, "Watch me."

He swooped down all around the skunk's head,
and the hummingbird swooped in real small
and got the ball out of his mouth
while the bluejay distracted him.

They went on and they scored the winning point.

The birds were so happy.

And Mr. Bluejay took all the credit—
he knew he was the one
that won that game.

So he went and he put a big sign hanging around all the trees
that said the birds are number one.

And if you go out in the woods today,
and you find a bluejay's nest,
you look:
and he'll have a piece of stringing hanging down
right in the bottom of it
as a signal to all the animals below
that the birds are number one. ✦

About This Story

For the Cherokee, stories hold cultural lessons, passing on important traditions from generation to generation. Yet, stories can change from storyteller to storyteller, and even from sitting to sitting.

This fluidity is captured by Dr. Barbara Duncan, a folklorist we interviewed at the Museum of the Cherokee Indian. Duncan uses a variety of methods in her book, *Living Legends of the*

Cherokee, to capture the oral traditions of Cherokee storytelling. Reading this version is akin to sitting in at Cherokee Elementary, listening to Kathi Smith Littlejohn relaying the story.

We love Littlejohn's retelling of this classic Cherokee story, which teaches us why the skunk has a stripe on his back and why the buzzard flies alone, for the way it illustrates the core Cherokee belief that even the smallest of creatures can make huge contributions.

That Good Old Mountain Dew

PRESENTED BY DOUG PRATT

My Uncle Bill had a still on the hill
Where he turned out a gallon or two.
  The buzzards in the sky
  Got so drunk they couldn't fly
When they smelled that old mountain dew.

(Chorus)
They call it that good old mountain dew
And them that refuse it are few.
  I'll shut up my mug
  If you'll fill up my jug
With that good old mountain dew.

My Uncle Bart he was sawed off and short.
He measured about four foot two.
  But he felt like a giant
  When you give him a pint
Of that good old mountain dew.

(Chorus)

My Aunt June had some fancy perfume
It had such a sweet smelling fume.
  Just imagine her surprise

When she had it analyzed
It was nothing but mountain dew.

(Chorus)

The preacher come by with his horse stepping high.
He said that his wife had the flu.
   I told him he ort
   Just to give her a snort
Of that good old mountain dew.

(Chorus) ✦

About This Story

Bluegrass, Folk, Americana: these musical traditions come from the music of the Appalachians. To mountain folk, music wasn't a commodity—it was an essential part of everyday life. And the banjo, one of the cheapest instruments to make in the early 1900s, became the essential sound of the region.

The National Park Service recognized a unique mountain culture would be lost during the formation of Great Smoky Mountains National Park, so they hired Joseph Hall, then a graduate student in linguistics at Columbia University, to document the soon-to-be-forgotten speech patterns of the Appalachians. Well, because Hall happened to be from Hollywood, mountain musicians were eager to play and be recorded for the project. Hall was the first person to record this rich musical culture, and went on to become known as "the Song Catcher."

"That Good Old Mountain Dew" is a classic song about the practice of turning corn into whiskey, or moonshining, which was illegal, but practiced widely. This version was presented at the Smokemont Campground in 1968 by seasonal ranger Doug Pratt. We found it in the oral history collection at Gatlinburg's Anna Porter Public Library. Feel free to have a sip as you sing along—making up your own tune is half the fun!

A Valley of Memories

JOHN PARRIS

The valley is always in their hearts.

It is a love they cherish unto themselves and champion to all people.

And even though the land no longer belongs to them, they keep coming back—the Caldwells, the Hannahs, the Palmers, the Rogers, the Woodys.

For their roots go deep in Cataloochee soil.

They were born and raised in the valley. Their kith and kin are buried here.

They have a story and a legend for every foot of ground.

And the ruts of the little dirt track that winds along the creek is as familiar as beloved wrinkles.

But the valley of their upbringing has changed.

There are only ghosts here now, and memories.

Smoke no longer signals to smoke from placid chimneys. The hearth-fires are dead. The cabins are gone, like the people, like the cattle and sheep and hogs.

And yet they keep coming back—the old, the very old, and the not-so-old. Back from cities and towns and faraway places.

They come back to "reune" at the old church for singing and dinner-on-the-ground.

They come back to visit the site of the old homeplace, to walk the old familiar trails, to wander among the headstones in the little graveyards, to show their grandchildren where their grand sires grooved together a cabin, or just to sit a spell beside the singing stream.

They come back to the valley with mixed feelings.

For through their joy of returning time and again runs a thread of sadness and bitterness.

They remember how it used to be when they lived and laughed and played and combed the rich earth here.

And then they realize how it is now.

For the valley is no longer their valley. It is lost to them forever. A thing only to be looked upon, a place to be visited, a memory to hold from afar.

In the not too distant past, a time with which they all can identify, Cataloochee was a prosperous and thriving community of nearly a thousand people whose folks settled in here shortly after the American Revolution.

But then the federal government began annexing land for the Great Smoky Mountains National Park in the late 1930s, and the exodus out of the valley started.

Many an old settler fussed and cussed. And a few reckoned if they weren't so few they would take down their muzzle-loaders and make a fight of it.

But they had to go. And they went without shedding a drop of blood. They packed up their housen goods, rounded up their stock, and moved out of the valley and down the mountain.

With them they carried a feeling for the valley that nothing ever would kill or destroy or change.

They went knowing that they were leaving behind more than just some far-off high mountain land.

They were leaving a way of life and long memories.

For the valley had been home as long as they could remember. It had been home to their mothers and fathers, their grandparents and great-grandparents.

High and wild and isolated, a real shut-in of a place, the valley had grown and prospered unto itself.

Here they knew an independence and a freedom they would never again know.

Here they had loved and laughed and were beholden to no man.

There was game in the forest about them—deer and bear and wild turkeys—and the streams rippled with trout.

Here they had been self-sufficient, living off the land's fat, needing nothing store-bought except maybe a little coffee and salt, lead and powder.

They seldom left the valley, for the road out was a winding, twisting dirt track that was practically impassable in a wagon during the winter. And the years have improved it little.

They had their churches, and they had a school.

The buildings still stand as silent reminders of another era.

Once a year the folks whose roots go deep in Cataloochee earth gather at the Palmer Chapel Methodist Church for their annual reunion when there is worship service and singing.

It's always the second Sunday in August.

They come with their song books and baskets of food.

And when they've finished their service and had dinner-on-the-ground, the families start pairing off and taking off up the creek or down the creek or up the hollow to visit the site of the old homeplace.

Even though only a couple of the old places are left, among them the old Woody Home, the springs are still there, and they go there to drink again of the cold, sweet water.

Some go off into the weed-grown orchards to pick an apple from a tree that Great-grandpa Woody set out more than a hundred years ago.

Others take off up the creek-trail where the poplars and hemlock stand like sentinels—virgin giants 16-feet around that were old when the first folks settled in her.

And after they've visited up and down the valley, they head for home beyond the Cataloochee Divide, off across the mountains there.

But, God willing, they'll come back.

For the homing note is still here. ✦

About This Story

Great Smoky Mountains National Park was the first national park in the southeastern United States. Creating this park protected the beautiful Appalachian Mountains from the private logging interests that were decimating the landscape. But it was also a complex endeavor, and the descendants who live in the region continue to experience the pain of their families' eviction.

Parris's poem captures the complex legacy of Cataloochee Valley, a place that once served as home, and an entire way of life, in the Appalachians. Still, many individuals are grateful to see the National Park Service preserving the land as they remember it from their youth. They know that their "homing note" will remain, and welcome the millions of visitors who want to share in the experience of this place.

The Removed Townhouses

FREEMAN OWLE

I have probably one more that I'd like to do today.
And this is sort of a revelation-type story in Cherokee history.
And I don't understand exactly how it originated,
  but evidently long before the tragedies of the people happened,
  the Cherokees were sitting in a council house.
And you can imagine this big building sitting on top of a mound
  of the ancient mound builders
  with thousands of seats inside.
And they're all gathered in the middle of winter,
  and there's a big fire crackling in the middle of the council.
And the chiefs are all gathered
  in the center,
  at the bottom,
  and the people are listening
  to the oral history being told
  or to the business being discussed.
When all of a sudden
  with no wind whatsoever outside
  the bearskin on the council house opens up
  wide enough for a person to come through
  and then sort of folds back,
  and then all of a sudden
  drops back into place.

The Cherokee, being very superstitious
    as they were in those days,
    realized that someone, some spirit,
    had entered the council house.
So they sat very quietly,
    and sure enough, up in the corner of the council house
    they began to see a light.
A sort of greenish-colored light materialized,
    and it soon turned into a person.
They knew this person was a Cherokee,
    but they didn't know who he was.
He came down to where the chiefs were sitting,
    and he said,
    "You, my brothers and sisters, must follow me.
    For out of the east will come a group of people
    who will destroy your homes.
    And your villages will be burned,
    and your children will be killed,
    and your homeland will be taken away,
    and never again will you be happy."
And so the Cherokee said,
    "No, we can't leave,
    because this land belonged to my mothers' mothers' mother."
He said,
    "I'll be back in seven days,
    and you must fast and decide
    whether you'll go with me
    or stay here and suffer."
In seven days he came back again,
    and half of the people had decided to follow him,
    half had decided to stay home.
And so when he came,
    the half that followed him

went up toward the mountain,
   the sacred mountain of the Cherokee.
And he got to this great massive rock cliff
   and he touched it with his hand,
   and the whole cliff opened up.
And you could hear people singing and laughing inside the mountain,
   and a stairwell leading up to a beautiful land
   of springtime and summer.
The people began to march in
   with the butterflies flying,
   and the fruit trees bearing fruit,
   and the people were all happy.
One man at the end
   decided that—he had left his family there in the village,
   and he wanted to go back and get them
   and bring them to this beautiful land.
He rushed back to the village
   and headed back to the mountain.
When he got back to the mountain with his family
   the mountain had closed up,
   and they said he was crazy
   and left him there alone.
He stayed there for seven days,
   and on the seventh day
   he began to hear the singing
   deep within the earth.
And so he went back to the village.
And from that day forward
   he told the people in the village
   that if you're quiet enough,
      long enough,
and if you sit and listen to the streams
and really are aware

and very quiet and still,

that you too can hear the people singing within the earth,

    those happy ones that went on before.

And sure enough, the settlers came,

    and they began to burn the villages

    and take away the land.

And the Cherokee people have been searching

    for that happiness

    they had long, long ago.

Even today, we have things coming into the reservations

    that make the people not so happy.

It never ends.

And I think the teaching of this story

    not only was the fact that there was a revelation

    of what was about to happen—

    people losing their homeland

    on the Trail of Tears and so on.

But also to teach us

    that we should never let the child disappear from us.

You remember when you were a child,

    when you would take off your shoes

    and prod through the mud puddles

    and laugh and sing?

Remember when you were a child,

    that not a butterfly passed

    that you didn't see it and chase it?

And not an animal or an insect were overlooked,

    that you were so close to nature

    and so close to Mother Earth

    that those were the things that were important to you?

So as we grow older we began to,

    in this day in time,

    sit in front of the e-mail for hours, the computer screen,

and we don't know where our children are;
the rest of our families send their grandparents to the old folks'
    home
and turn on the TV, a one-sided interaction.
And we should remain like children
    and keep society from choking us and strangling us
    to the point of heart attacks and high blood pressure.
We should remain like children
    and sometimes take our shoes off
    and prod through the mud puddles
    and sit by the streams
    and listen to the talking of the streams
        and the whispers of the wind.
And save ourselves a great deal of medical bills
    and psychological analysis
    and relaxation therapy,
    which costs fifty to a hundred dollars an hour.
Go listen to the stream.
He'll talk to you and will not charge you a penny.
So I think this is Cherokee psychology,
    studied and revised for thousands of years.
I think it's good for all of us.
We must preserve the earth,
    and we must value the lives of our elders
    and the lives of our children
    and save them a place to live.
If we don't
    then there will be a revelation for the people of today
    as well as for the Cherokee.
Thank you. ✦

About This Story

The eviction of the Cherokee occurred almost one hundred years before the eviction memorialized in Parris's poem. The Indian Removal Act of 1830 forced Cherokee peoples to give up their lands east of the Mississippi River, and resettle in present-day Oklahoma. Their route from North Carolina to Oklahoma became known as the Trail of Tears.

But the Cherokee story doesn't end there. Through wit and determination, the Eastern Band of Cherokee Indians were able to purchase the Qualla Boundary, a territory that borders the southern entrance to Great Smoky Mountains National Park. Today, they continue to govern the territory as a sovereign nation.

Owle's story is just one account of this great tragedy. What we find surprising are Owle's modern gripes—email, computers, TV. They may not be what you associate with American Indians, but the poem is a great reminder of what we heard again and again from individuals we spoke to across the country—the Cherokee people were the first on this land and despite all the hardships, they have never left. They are still here, and here they thrive.

When a small little chap . . .

WILEY OAKLEY

Tramp the trails of the Smoky Mountains land lissen to the soft whispering winds on a summer day and sometimes these soft whispering winds can be heard in the early part of May while tramping through the Great Smoky Mountains far back in the wild woods many miles away.

Now I wish to take you back to my boyhood days 40 years ago when I first started out to ramble the woods of the mountains. A dog and a gun and then a lantern light to hunt at night, beleave me I was a very happy boy at the age of 14 I could fire a gun like no bad business and how for a boy at this age. When I looked through the site on the gun barrel, taking a good fine bead sited on the wild animals of any kind, or birds the same, I pulled the trigger and then the rore from the gun. When the smoke had vanashed away then I looked to the spot to fiend my meet lying on the ground stone dead, and it was very seldom I ever made a miss as I had trained myself as a gunman of the woods. I would also repair guns but the kind of guns was the cap and ball gun and the people of the mountains called the guns hogrifles. Old fashing muzzle loading guns take some time to load. One of these guns You had to be a very good shot otherwise one shot would be all you could get at the animal or bird and the game was gone by the time you would load the gun for the second shot.

Now I will take you back to my first hunt when a small little chap as I was born and raised up at the foot of Mt. LeConte. My father was one of the old bear hunters and trappers. At that time, when I was only 5 or 6 years old, father would sit around the fireside at cold nights too cold to hunt. Father would tell these hair raising storys about his advinchers in the heep big mountains of the Smokys, and the two good hunting dogs he had. I had seen all the fir skins that father would bring in and stretch on wooden boards, hued out to fit the skins of different kinds of animals. After I had seen and heard all of these things I made up my mind one day . . . in the evening I would take these two dogs out for a hunt. What a load of animals I could bring in home to show father and the rest of the family. The dogs names was Trail and Troop. In the evening I slipped out at the back door of the cabin, calling up old trail and troop. At first the dogs dident want to follow me off to the woods. So I then thought of another way of taking these dogs away from home to hunt. I made my way back to the kitchen and found a large peace of corn bread. In the mountains at that time the people called it corn pone. Corn pone was baked in an oven or in an open fireplace, baking 2 large pones of bread at once. So I found one of these large pones of corn bread and out to the back I went to where the dogs was. I said, Now come, trail and troop, I have something you will like and if you dogs will follow me off to the wild woods I will give you this bread. So the trick did work. I would only give the dogs a small peace of this corn bread just now and then as the dogs and I travelled off into the dark woods.

Soon we reached the tall timber, soon the bread gave out, but by this time the dogs began to hunt and the Sun bent low in the evening. Soon the dogs struck the trail of some kind of an animal and soon they fell to barking. I went on in the direction where I could heare the sound of these dogs. Soon I found the dogs, they had something tred under large rocks so I thought heare is the place where we will catch some kind of a wild animal. Then I sat on the rocks and waited thinking soon the dogs will scratch out the animal and kill it but soon dark come on and I began to cry in tiers. What will I do, dark is on, and I am not sure witch way is my home. Then I desided to spend the night wright heare, picking out a large flat rock then I called up the dogs on this rock. I put my arms around the dogs neck and pulled them closet to my side and how these dogs seemed to know I was frightened and afraid that I might not see the light of another day. What would my father think of my not coming home. By this time the night got darker and darker til you couldent see your hand before your face as I was in heavy timbers of himlocks trees with their everygreen bows made the night darker. But I pulled the dogs closer and the warmth from the dogs kept me from freezing through the night.

Sometime in the night I fell aslep with my arms around the dogs. There was a mistery about these two dogs. They seamed to know I was lost and was to small to be out hunting in the wild mountains. These 2 dogs was highly praised by my father and at one time he was offered a good milk cow for one of them but father would not trade at any price. But the night rolled on while I sleep between the 2 dogs so still and quiet on the same rock where I had planned to spend the night 3 or 4 miles away from my home. At that time there were many wild animals that could have soon taken my life but these two dogs was taking good care of the lad who had started out to make a hunter so young and small. Sometime in the night all at once the dogs made a dash from the rock and I was waken from my sleep. A strange feling came over me thinking what had happened to the dogs that they had dash from where I had been asleep and all the thing that I could think of was some great animal had come around and scared the dogs away and it must be a bear or some other dangurous animal. I looked to see if anything was coming neare but the night was dark. I couldent see at all and at the same time I hadent felt any teeth or claws bite me from any side, but how soon it may be I will be eaten up I dident know. I could still heare the rushing of the dogs in the underbrush and leaves. The barking I could heare but all at once the dogs seemed to hush, I looked in the drection the dogs had gone and I saw a light coming towarde me. Soon the dogs come back to where I was sitting on the large rock. They climbed up barking and whining and soon my Older Brother came up and was I glad to see him at that time. So I climbed around my brothers neck and was carried through the woods and back again safe and sound. All the family was glad to have me home. My father said it was a wonder that I was found that same night. So many things could of happened to me and I must not never try this again. I had give them plenty of trouble that night. That night they had sent out someone on all the different trails that led into the mountains and for the boys to look for the footprints or the dogs in all soft spots about the water, and the same time lissen for the barking of the dogs and if they meet the dogs coming in home then go the direction the dogs had come from and then they would fiend the lost boy. Now I was the youngest boy of 8 but this was my first hunt in life and last one for some 3 or fore, after this I would hunt with father or some of my older brothers.

As I was the youngest of 8 and was reared up without any mother my oldest brothers wife said she had to take the place of my mother for a few years. My mother died when I was a small boy. My father said many times that I had more ways like the Indians than a little and father repeted these sayings up til his deth about 20 years ago from the date of this book 1940. My father and his people came across the waters from Scotland landing in Bostin, Mass. many years ago. My grandfather Oakley went from England to Scotland and met my grandmother and married her and then they all came across to U.S.A. My father said they came down for a few years, and his older brothers began down for a few years, and his older brother began to marry and scatter off in different parts of the country. My father was the youngest of 8. They moved to Knoxville when father was only 11 years old and lived there for a while. The Sivel war come on and they desided to moave up in the Smoky mountains. As the war was growing strong at the time father said he would visit the mountain peoples homes and sometimes carry in wood and help out the women folks as the most of the men was gone to war. Finally he fell in love with a Indian girl or she was just part Indian and he married at the age of 16 and remained in the Great Smoky Mountains until his deth. And now I am writing these true storys as best as I know how and no dought this book will be different from any other book on the Smoky Mountains as the writer spent all my life among the heep big mountains, as the Indians sometimes say. At the same time I havent had the opportunity of being schooled like the young people today. All I have ever known is to ramble the great Smoky Mountains. What little I know is all picked up, you might say I am a self made man if there is such a thing. You see I know very little about the outer world and City life but I can tell you all about the outdoor life in the Great Smoky Mountains and I picked up botany from people who teaches botany and bird life from people who study birds and if these prof.s. is wrong then Im wrong so we all fall in the ditch together.

Nature is one of the studies in the Great Smoky Mountains that every purson should know something about. She is a wonderful study. So I advise every pursen who reads this little book just take time to stroll out on some of these beautiful trails and every now and then take a look and lissen and take a deep breath and look things over. It dont make any different how young or old you may be jus go at a slow pace and try to forget about time or other worry. When you are in the mountains do like the Roamin' Man of the Mountain do. Time and money dont mean anything. Most of the mountain people thinks about the same thing about this rushing business. ✦

About This Story

An authentic Appalachian guide, Wiley Oakley was at home in the mountains of blue smoke. Like other local families, his grandfather migrated to Tennessee from Scotland. But Oakley stood out in a town full of vibrant characters. As one of the first mountain guides for the Great Smoky Mountains National Park, he showed the region to hundreds of curious tourists from around the world.

One of Wiley Oakley's sayings when discussing his book was "I've never been to school so I didn't put in these colons and semi-colons. All I put was a period. And that means, catch your breath and start again."

We commend the original editor of this collection of Oakley's stories, who knew that leaving the writing unedited best captured the experience of conversing with Oakley. And it's that style that embodies so much of the beauty of the lost mountain culture—despite not being educated in a traditional schoolroom, Oakley's is a voice that bursts with a deep wisdom of the landscape, and a vibrant sense of life in spite of the mountain hardships. His unique upbringing informs a hard-earned wisdom, one that makes us listen when he advises "every pursen who reads this little book [to] just take time to stroll out on some of these beautiful trails and every now and then take a look and lissen and take a deep breath and look things over."

ROCKY MOUNTAIN NATIONAL PARK

A Place for the Wild

SPLIT BY the Continental Divide, Rocky Mountain National Park is a wilderness park bursting with megafauna, scenic vistas, more than 350 trails (many in the backcountry), and Trail Ridge Road: the highest continuous highway in the country leading visitors into the alpine tundra at 12,183 feet.

illustration by
EMILY DOVE

efore we made our way from the Great Smoky Mountains in Tennessee to the Rocky Mountains of Colorado, we had to confirm one thing. While our Nashville Airbnb host went about their day around the house as usual, we anxiously huddled in our bedroom and awaited the results of our pregnancy test. Was Ilyssa just feeling sick in the Smokies, or was it something else? We took a peek at the test: we were very pregnant.

This wasn't unwelcome news, but it also wasn't quite something we were expecting to hear three weeks into a four-month road trip. Can you hike while pregnant? Would camping be safe? Was our trip even possible anymore? We phoned a friend, a new mom, to learn what her experience was like, and went into town to buy a book on pregnancy.

The drive from Tennessee to Colorado is made up of long stretches of flat land. The sheer immenseness of the country served as a dramatic backdrop for thinking about our unexpected news and the journey ahead, both in the next four months and for the rest of our lives. On the morning we learned our baby was the size of a poppy seed, we sat staring at our morning bagel in disbelief. Unsure if we could even continue the trip, we scheduled our first OB/GYN visit for Denver, Colorado, and decided to save any decision-making until then. So for now, it was on with the project.

As we drove into the gateway town of Estes Park, the view of the snow-capped Rocky Mountains told us we had arrived. And to our right, the herds of elk wandering the golf courses reminded us we were in a wild place. Rocky Mountain National Park was established in 1915, one year before the National Park Service was created to manage the country's growing collection of public lands. In Estes Park, Enos Mills, mountain guide and friend of John Muir, was the most visible feature of the national park movement, and he traveled to places like San Francisco, Kansas City, and Chicago to give lectures on the importance of preservation of the wild. Though Mills is often credited as the Father of Rocky Mountain National Park, many others also contributed to the effort. Isabella Bird, a British traveler, published letters from her visit to Estes Park over thirty years before the park was created—letters that captured the imaginations of people across the world. There was also F.O. Stanley, inventor and hotelier—whose Estes Park hotel inspired Stephen King's novel *The Shining*—and groups like the Estes Park

Woman's Club and the Colorado Mountain Club who raised funds and donated land to the park effort. Behind this park, as with all our parks, was a community effort to preserve these lands forever.

The Rockies were proposed as a wilderness area in the 1970s and designated as wilderness in 2009. It remains 95 percent wilderness today, home to elk, moose, bighorn sheep, and a handful of black bears. As a wilderness, the construction of roads or other development is limited, making the park a haven for backcountry hikers, skiers, and mountain climbers looking for solitude. This designation also influences the management of the park. Moraine Park once hosted lodges and a golf course, but all were torn down to return the landscape to nature. Local historian Curt Buchholtz toured us around a number of historic sites—the Elkhorn Lodge that housed Colorado's first park ranger, the site of Lord Dunraven's very first tourist lodge, Enos Mills's and Isabella Bird's cabins—all of which sit outside the park, without fanfare. The emphasis of this park is not its human history: it's the wild.

While a marmot in the alpine tundra certainly is eager to bark a story at you, it was the human stories we were interested in finding, from those indigenous to these lands to the stories of today. An important part of our process was to collect stories from underrepresented people in each of the national parks we visited, and the Rocky Mountains challenged our persistence. The Ute and Arapaho tribes, who were native to this region, were nomadic. They hunted in these mountains, but settled elsewhere to escape the harsh winters. There was little Ute or Arapaho presence in the nearby towns we visited, except for an occasional mention of the famous Arapaho pack trip of 1914, organized by Harriet Vaille and Edna Hendrie of the Colorado Mountain Club. They sought to strengthen the case for preservation to Congress by reviving traditional Arapaho place names. Ironically, it was the Ute tribes, not the Arapaho, that had a longer history in the land, but the Ute elders rejected the Colorado Mountain Club's invitation due to legends of a tragedy at Grand Lake, on the west side of the park, which left hundreds of women and children dead. Without a local organization that interprets the Ute or Arapaho history and culture, the native legacies of the Rocky Mountains remain difficult to access.

European settlers faced difficulties soon after they arrived in the Rockies in the 1850s. Miners on the west side panned for gold, only to find that there was none. The short growing season of roughly 40 days resulted in the saying that "all you can grow around here is radishes, pansies, and hell." The primary business of the early settlers soon turned to providing lodging for the visitors who flocked to the Rockies each summer. Abner Sprague, one of the first settlers, said, "We came here for small ranch operations, but guests and visitors became so numerous, at first wanting eggs, milk, and other provisions, then wanting lodging, and finally demanding full accommodations, that we had to go into the hotel business or go bankrupt from keeping free company!"

At least until Memorial Day, when room rates quadrupled, we happily took up lodging in the Rockies, enjoying showers, washing machines, and nearby bathrooms. The other physical challenges of the Rockies made the comforts of a hotel all the more enticing. In these mountains, visitors are somewhere between 7,522 to 14,259 feet (at the top of Longs Peak) above sea level. Thin mountain air becomes a shortness of breath for East Coasters like us. And altitude sickness is made worse during a first-trimester pregnancy.

Though we were there at the start of summer, our visit just coincided with the opening of Trail Ridge Road. Setting the record for the highest continuous highway in the United States, Trail Ridge Road offers visitors access to the dramatic alpine tundra within the park as well as the Alpine Visitor Center, the country's highest at 11,796 feet. When we arrived, it was just being dug out from a snow pile higher than the building itself and the electricity had yet to be turned on. Long branches and poles, serving as guides for snow plows, flanked the roads. At this elevation, you will find an unforgiving, yet fragile, landscape with thin soil, intense ultraviolet light, bitter cold, and unpredictable weather that can change suddenly—a sunny day gives way to a windy thunderstorm, a clear afternoon turns into a hazy mist. The Rockies are also home to the Continental Divide. Water that falls west of the Divide flows to the Pacific Ocean, while water that falls east reaches the Atlantic. Strolling the River Trail in Estes Park, we were in awe of the river's forceful and rapid flow—a visual reminder of snowmelt in the mountains. This snowmelt is an important source of water across all of the United States. For farmers in the lower plains, thousands of miles away, this water is a vital lifeline for their crops. Managing it is so important that it has become political. They say in the Rockies that "whiskey's for drinking, but water's for fighting."

In a doctor's office in Denver, our first appointment since our positive pregnancy test, we got our first glimpse of our little stowaway—a barely distinguishable speck with a glittering heartbeat. Amused by all of our questions, the doctor walked us through what we could expect and reminded us of all the various environments and situations in which people have babies—in deserts and jungles, on mountains, and yes, living out of a tent. We quickly realized that while we had finally gotten our footing and established a solid process for our research, we were about to take on the whole new challenge of organizing doctor appointments in different states every four weeks, buying and eating healthy food with limited options for groceries and zero access to refrigeration, and not sharing the biggest news of our life with anyone. This was a challenge that was well worth it, and so our search for stories was still on.

The Rocky Mountain National Park Colorado

CHARLES EDWIN HEWES

pread a magnificent wilderness of mountain crags forever lifted unto the bright eyes of the beaming stars; of foaming waters issuing from glistening fields of snow and ice, and gathered and pooled in lakes reflecting peak and spire in skies of melting azure; of streams forever clasped in the arms of the brooding forest and foam-flecked gorge; place mountain meadows sweet and odorous with the scent of lilies, of roses, of orchids rare and delicate; clothe broad alpine slopes with soft green coats of fragrant balsam, pine, fir, and aspen, and populate them with bighorn, deer, elk, bear, beaver, cougar, wolf, and the other quadruped multitudes of the *oberland*; fill the streams with the play and flash of silvery-finned companies; in the dizzy reaches of the uplifted skies place the American eagle enthroned among the clouds; and in the low recesses of valley, of cañon, glade and wood, place wing and voice of the ecstatic lark and thrush and other innumerable and melodious warblers of sylvan song, and with them the diaphanous winged myriads of an insect world of brilliant moth and butterfly, and where the wild bee hoards honeyed treasures supped from blooms of ravishing beauty; then in the heart of this teeming wonderland, piercing the very bosom of the empyrean, stand one great peak—a glorious shaft of gleaming granite—so noble, so vast in its overwhelming beetling solitude of grandeur that the spectacle stills the very heart with infinite awe; then over all, from the great peak's lofty brow down to the depths of the shining stream-paved bed of the deepest cañon, dash the golden beams of a Colorado sunrise summoning the mountain world to the shrine of a perfect day—this is Longs Peak in the midst of the Rocky Mountain National Park; this is the crest of the American continent, the heart of the Rocky Mountains; here is the beauty, the inspiration, the romance, of Denver's Great-White-Way—her two hundred miles of peerless mountains—the Snowy Range! ✦

About This Story

Many of Colorado's first residents arrived on doctor's orders. The treatment for tuberculosis at the turn of the twentieth century was fresh, dry air with lots of sunlight, and a hearty diet. Many of these "lung-ers" sought the clean, crisp air of the Rocky Mountains in Colorado. And many lung-ers, like Freelan Oscar Stanley, inventor of the Stanley Steamer automobile and founder of the Stanley Hotel, would go on to recover and fall in love with the Rockies. P. T. Barnum noted that "2 out of every 3 people is coming here to die, and when they get here, they find they can't do it!"

Lush meadows, clean water, and abundant beauty are the hallmarks of this region, and early residents of Estes Park just fell into the hospitality business. Estes Park has continued down this path, growing from 6,000 residents during the off-season to 25,000 residents each summer, with lodging as the primary industry. Hewes's introduction boasts of the dramatic scenes that eager tourists seek in the Rocky Mountains.

Excerpt from *A Lady's Life in the Rocky Mountains*

Letter VII

ISABELLA BIRD

Estes Park, Colorado, October

As this account of the ascent of Long's Peak could not be written at the time, I am much disinclined to write it, especially as no sort of description within my powers could enable another to realize the glorious sublimity, the majestic solitude, and the unspeakable awfulness and fascination of the scenes in which I spent Monday, Tuesday, and Wednesday.

Long's Peak, 14,700 feet high, blocks up one end of Estes Park, and dwarfs all the surrounding mountains. From it on this side rise, snow-born, the bright St. Vrain, and the Big and Little Thompson. By sunlight or moonlight its splintered grey crest is the one object which, in spite of wapiti and bighorn, skunk and grizzly, unfailingly arrests the eyes. From it come all storms of snow and wind, and the forked lightnings play round its head like a glory. It is one of the noblest of mountains, but in one's imagination it grows to be much more than a mountain. It becomes invested with a personality. In its caverns and shyness one comes to fancy that it generates and chains the strong winds, to let them loose in its fury. The thunder becomes its voice, and the lightnings do it homage. Other summits blush under the morning kiss of the sun, and turn pale the next moment; but it detains the first sunlight and holds it round its head for an hour at least, till it please to change from rosy red to deep blue; and the sunset, as if spell-bound, lingers latest on its crest. The soft winds which hardly rustle the pine needles down here are raging rudely up there round its motionless summit. The mark of fires is upon it; and though it has passed into a grim repose, it tells of fire and upheaval as truly, though not as eloquently, as the living volcanoes of Hawaii. Here under its shadow one learns how naturally nature worship, and the propitiation of the forces of nature, arose in minds which had no better light.

Long's Peak, "the American Matterhorn," as some call it, was ascended five years ago for the first time. I thought I should like to attempt it, but up to Monday, when Evans left for Denver, cold water was thrown upon the project. It was too late in the season, the winds were likely to be strong, etc.; but just before leaving, Evans said that the weather was looking more settled, and if I did not get farther than the timber line it would be worth going. Soon after he left, "Mountain Jim" came in, and he would go up as guide, and the two youths who rode here with me from Longmount and I caught at the proposal. Mrs. Edwards at once baked bread for three days, steaks were cut from the steer which hangs up conveniently, and tea, sugar, and butter were benevolently added. Our picnic was not to be a luxurious or "well-found" one, for, in order to avoid the expense of a pack mule, we limited our luggage to what our saddle horses could carry. Behind my saddle I carried three pair of camping blankets and a quilt, which reached to my shoulders. My own boots were so much worn that it was painful to walk, even about the park, in them, so Evans had lent me a pair of his hunting boots, which hung to the horn of my saddle. The horses of the two young men were equally loaded, for we had to prepare for many degrees of frost. "Jim" was a shocking figure; he had on an old pair of high boots, with a baggy pair of old trousers made of deer hide, held on by an old scarf tucked into them; a leather shirt, with three or four ragged unbuttoned waistcoats over it; an old smashed wideawake, from under which his tawny, neglected ringlets hung; and with his one eye, his one long spur, his knife in his belt, his revolver in his waistcoat pocket, his saddle covered with an old beaver skin, from which the paws hung down; his camping blankets behind him, and his axe, canteen, and other gear hanging to the horn, he was as awful-looking a ruffian as one could see. By way of contrast he rode a small Arab mare, of exquisite beauty, skittish, high spirited, gentle, but altogether too light for him, and he fretted her incessantly to make her display herself.

Heavily loaded as all our horses were, "Jim" started over the half-mile of level grass at a hard gallop, and then throwing his mare on her haunches, pulled up alongside of me, and with a grace of manner which soon made me forget his appearance, entered into a conversation which lasted for more than three hours, in spite of the manifold checks of fording streams, single file, abrupt ascents and descents, and other incidents of mountain travel. The ride was one series of glories and surprises, of "park" and glade, of lake and stream, of mountains on mountains, culminating in the rent pinnacles of Long's Peak, which looked yet grander and ghastlier as we crossed an attendant mountain 11,000 feet high. The slanting sun added fresh beauty every hour. There were dark pines against a lemon sky, grey peaks reddening and etherealizing, gorges of deep and infinite blue, floods of golden glory pouring through canyons of enormous depth, an atmosphere of absolute purity, an occasional foreground of cotton-wood and aspen flaunting in red and gold to intensify the blue gloom of the pines, the trickle and murmur of streams fringed with icicles, the strange *sough* of gusts moving among the pine tops—sights and sounds not of the lower earth, but of the solitary, beast-haunted, frozen upper altitudes. From the dry, buff grass of Estes Park we turned off up a trail on the side of a pine-hung gorge, up a steep pine-clothed hill, down to a small valley, rich in fine, sun-cured hay about eighteen inches high, and enclosed by high mountains whose deepest hollow contains a lily-covered lake, fitly named "The Lake of the Lilies." Ah, how magical its beauty was, as it slept in silence, while *there* the dark pines were mirrored motionless in its pale gold, and *here* the great white lily cups and dark green leaves rested on amethyst-colored water!

From this we ascended into the purple gloom of great pine forests which clothe the skirts of the mountains up to a height of about 11,000 feet, and from their chill and solitary depths we had glimpses of golden atmosphere and rose-lit summits, not of "the land very far off," but of the land nearer now in all its grandeur, gaining in sublimity by nearness—glimpses, too, through a broken vista of purple gorges, of the illimitable Plains lying idealized in the late sunlight, their baked, brown expanse transfigured into the likeness of a sunset sea rolling infinitely in waves of misty gold.

We rode upwards through the gloom on a steep trail blazed through the forest, all my intellect concentrated on avoiding being dragged off my horse by impending branches, or having the blankets badly torn, as those of my companions were, by sharp dead limbs, between which there was hardly room to pass—the horses breathless, and requiring to stop every few yards, though their riders, except myself, were afoot. The gloom of the dense, ancient, silent forest is to me awe inspiring. On such an evening it is soundless, except for the branches creaking in the soft wind, the frequent snap of decayed timber, and a murmur in the pine tops as of a not distant waterfall, all tending to produce *eeriness* and a sadness "hardly akin to pain." There no lumberer's axe has ever rung. The trees die when they have attained their prime, and stand there, dead and bare, till the fierce mountain winds lay them prostrate. The pines grew smaller and more sparse as we ascended, and the last stragglers wore a tortured, warring look. The timber line was passed, but yet a little higher a slope of mountain meadow dipped to the south-west towards a bright stream trickling under ice and icicles, and there a grove of the beautiful silver spruce marked our camping ground. The trees were in miniature, but so exquisitely arranged that one might well ask what artist's hand had planted them, scattering them here, clumping them there, and training their slim spires towards heaven. Hereafter, when I call up memories of the glorious, the view from this camping ground will come up. Looking east, gorges opened to the distant Plains, then fading into purple grey. Mountains with pine-clothed skirts rose in ranges, or, solitary, uplifted their grey summits, while close behind, but nearly 3,000 feet above us, towered the bald white crest of Long's Peak, its huge precipices red with the light of a sun long lost to our eyes. Close to us, in the caverned side of the Peak, was snow that, owing to its position, is eternal. Soon the afterglow came on, and before it faded a big half-moon hung out of the heavens, shining through the silver blue foliage of the pines on the frigid background of snow, and turning the whole into fairyland. The "photo" which accompanies this letter is by a courageous Denver artist who attempted the ascent just before I arrived, but, after camping out at the timber line for a week, was foiled by the perpetual storms, and was driven down again, leaving some very valuable apparatus about 3,000 feet from the summit.

Unsaddling and picketing the horses securely, making the beds of pine shoots, and dragging up logs for fuel, warmed us all. "Jim" built up a great fire, and before long we were all sitting around it at supper. It didn't matter much that we had to drink our tea out of the battered meat tins in which it was boiled, and eat strips of beef reeking with pine smoke without plates or forks.

· ✦ ·

The mercury at 9 P.M. was 12° below the freezing point. "Jim," after a last look at the horses, made a huge fire, and stretched himself out beside it, but "Ring" lay at my back to keep me warm. I could not sleep, but the night passed rapidly. I was anxious about the ascent, for gusts of ominous sound swept through the pines at intervals. Then wild animals howled, and "Ring" was perturbed in spirit about them. Then it was strange to see the notorious desperado, a red-handed man, sleeping as quietly as innocence sleeps. But, above all, it was exciting to lie there, with no better shelter than a bower of pines, on a mountain 11,000 feet high, in the very heart of the Rocky Range, under twelve degrees of frost, hearing sounds of wolves, with shivering stars looking through the fragrant canopy, with arrowy pines for bed-posts, and for a night lamp the red flames of a camp-fire.

Day dawned long before the sun rose, pure and lemon colored. The rest were looking after the horses, when one of the students came running to tell me that I must come farther down the slope, for "Jim" said he had never seen such a sunrise. From the chill, grey Peak above, from the everlasting snows, from the silvered pines, down through mountain ranges with their depths of Tyrian purple, we looked to where the Plains lay cold, in blue-grey, like a morning sea against a far horizon. Suddenly, as a dazzling streak at first, but enlarging rapidly into a dazzling sphere, the sun wheeled above the grey line, a light and glory as when it was first created. "Jim" involuntarily and reverently uncovered his head, and exclaimed, "I believe there is a God!" I felt as if, Parsee-like, I must worship. The grey of the Plains changed to purple, the sky was all one rose-red flush, on which vermilion cloud-streaks rested; the ghastly peaks gleamed like rubies, the earth and heavens were new created. Surely "the Most High dwelleth not in temples made with hands!" For a full hour those Plains simulated the ocean, down to whose limitless expanse of purple, cliff, rocks, and promontories swept down.

By seven we had finished breakfast, and passed into the ghastlier solitudes above, I riding as far as what, rightly or wrongly, are called the "Lava Beds," an expanse of large and small boulders, with snow in their crevices. It was very cold; some water which we crossed was frozen hard enough to bear the horse. "Jim" had advised me against taking any wraps, and my thin Hawaiian riding dress, only fit for the tropics, was penetrated by the keen air. The rarefied atmosphere soon began to oppress our breathing, and I found that Evans's boots were so large that I had no foothold. Fortunately, before the real difficulty of the ascent began, we found, under a rock, a pair of small overshoes, probably left by the Hayden exploring expedition, which just lasted for the day. As we were leaping from rock to rock, "Jim" said, "I was thinking in the night about your traveling alone, and wondering where you carried your Derringer, for I could see no signs of it." On my telling him that I traveled unarmed, he could hardly believe it, and adjured me to get a revolver at once.

On arriving at the "Notch" (a literal gate of rock), we found ourselves absolutely on the knifelike ridge or backbone of Long's Peak, only a few feet wide, covered with colossal boulders and fragments, and on the other side shelving in one precipitous, snow-patched sweep of 3,000 feet to a picturesque hollow, containing a lake of pure green water. Other lakes, hidden among dense pine woods, were farther off, while close above us rose the Peak, which, for about 500 feet, is a smooth, gaunt, inaccessible-looking pile of granite. Passing through the "Notch," we looked along the nearly inaccessible side of the Peak, composed of boulder and *débris* of all shapes and sizes, through which appeared broad, smooth ribs of reddish-colored granite, looking as if they upheld the towering rock mass above. I usually dislike bird's-eye and panoramic views, but, though from a mountain, this was not one. Serrated ridges, not much lower than that on which we stood, rose, one beyond another, far as that pure atmosphere could carry the vision, broken into awful chasms deep with ice and snow, rising into pinnacles piercing the heavenly blue with their cold, barren grey, on, on for ever, till the most distant range upbore unsullied snow alone. There were fair lakes mirroring the dark pine woods, canyons dark and blue-black with unbroken expanses of pines, snow-slashed pinnacles, wintry heights frowning upon lovely parks, watered and wooded, lying in the lap of summer; North Park floating off into the blue distance, Middle Park closed till another season, the sunny slopes of Estes Park, and winding down among the mountains the snowy ridge of the Divide, whose bright waters seek both the Atlantic and Pacific Oceans. There far below, links of diamonds showed where the Grand River takes its rise to seek the mysterious Colorado, with its still unsolved enigma, and lose itself in the waters of the Pacific; and nearer the snow-born Thompson bursts forth from the ice to begin its journey to the Gulf of Mexico. Nature, rioting in her grandest mood, exclaimed with voices of grandeur, solitude, sublimity, beauty, and infinity, "Lord, what is man, that Thou art mindful of him? or the son of man, that Thou visitest him?" Never-to-be-forgotten glories they were, burnt in upon my memory by six succeeding hours of terror.

You know I have no head and no ankles, and never ought to dream of mountaineering; and had I known that the ascent was a real mountaineering feat I should not have felt the slightest ambition to perform it. As it is, I am only humiliated by my success, for "Jim" dragged me up, like a bale of goods, by sheer force of muscle. At the "Notch" the real business of the ascent began. Two thousand feet of solid rock towered above us, four thousand feet of broken rock shelved precipitously below; smooth granite ribs, with barely foothold, stood out here and there; melted snow refrozen several times, presented a more serious obstacle; many of the rocks were loose, and tumbled down when touched. To me it was a time of extreme terror. I was roped to "Jim," but it was of no use; my feet were paralyzed and slipped on the bare rock, and he said it was useless to try to go that way, and we retraced our steps. I wanted to return to the "Notch," knowing that my incompetence would detain the party, and one of the young men said almost plainly that a woman was a dangerous encumbrance, but the trapper replied shortly that if it were not to take a lady up he would not go up at all. He went on the explore, and reported that further progress on the correct line of ascent was blocked by ice; and then for two hours we descended, lowering ourselves by our hands from rock to rock along a boulder-strewn sweep of 4,000 feet, patched with ice and snow, and perilous from rolling stones. My fatigue, giddiness, and pain from bruised ankles, and arms half pulled out of their sockets, were so great that I should never have gone halfway had not "Jim," *nolens volens*, dragged me along with a patience and skill, and withal a determination that I should ascend the Peak, which never failed. After descending about 2,000 feet to avoid the ice, we got into a deep ravine with inaccessible sides, partly filled with ice and snow and partly with large and small fragments of rock, which were constantly giving away, rendering the footing very insecure. That part to me was two hours of painful and unwilling submission to the inevitable; of trembling, slipping, straining, of smooth ice appearing when it was least expected, and of weak entreaties to be left behind while the others went on. "Jim" always said that there was no danger, that there was only a short bad bit ahead, and that I should go up even if he carried me!

Slipping, faltering, gasping from the exhausting toil in the rareified air, with throbbing hearts and panting lungs, we reached the top of the gorge and squeezed ourselves between two gigantic fragments of rock by a passage called the "Dog's Lift," when I climbed on the shoulders of one man and then was hauled up. This introduced us by an abrupt turn round the south-west angle of the Peak to a narrow shelf of considerable length, rugged, uneven, and so overhung by the cliff in some places that it is necessary to crouch to pass at all. Above, the Peak looks nearly vertical for 400 feet; and below, the most tremendous precipice I have ever seen descends in one unbroken fall. This is usually considered the most dangerous part of the ascent, but it does not seem so to me, for such foothold as there is is secure, and one fancies that it is possible to hold on with the hands. But there, and on the final, and, to my thinking, the worst part of the climb, one slip, and a breathing, thinking, human being would lie 3,000 feet below, a shapeless, bloody heap! "Ring" refused to traverse the Ledge, and remained at the "Lift" howling piteously.

· ✦ ·

As we crept from the ledge round a horn of rock I beheld what made me perfectly sick and dizzy to look at—the terminal Peak itself—a smooth, cracked face or wall of pink granite, as nearly perpendicular as anything could well be up which it was possible to climb, well deserving the name of the "American Matterhorn."

Scaling, not climbing, is the correct term for this last ascent. It took one hour to accomplish 500 feet, pausing for breath every minute or two. The only foothold was in narrow cracks or on minute projections on the granite. To get a toe in these cracks, or here and there on a scarcely obvious projection, while crawling on hands and knees, all the while tortured with thirst and gasping and struggling for breath, this was the climb; but at last the Peak was won. A grand, well-defined mountain top it is, a nearly level acre of boulders, with precipitous sides all round, the one we came up being the only accessible one.

It was not possible to remain long. One of the young men was seriously alarmed by bleeding from the lungs, and the intense dryness of the day and the rarefication of the air, at a height of nearly 15,000 feet, made respiration very painful. There is always water on the Peak, but it was frozen as hard as a rock, and the sucking of ice and snow increases thirst. We all suffered severely from the want of water, and the gasping for breath made our mouths and tongues so dry that articulation was difficult, and the speech of all unnatural.

From the summit were seen in unrivalled combination all the views which had rejoiced our eyes during the ascent. It was something at last to stand upon the storm-rent crown of this lonely sentinel of the Rocky Range, on one of the mightiest of the vertebrae of the backbone of the North American continent, and to see the waters start for both oceans. Uplifted above love and hate and storms of passion, calm amidst the eternal silences, fanned by zephyrs and bathed in living blue, peace rested for that one bright day on the Peak, as if it were some region

Where falls not rain, or hail, or any snow,
Or ever wind blows loudly.

We placed our names, with the date of ascent, in a tin within a crevice, and descended to the Ledge, sitting on the smooth granite, getting our feet into cracks and against projections, and letting ourselves down by our hands, "Jim" going before me, so that I might steady my feet against his powerful shoulders. I was no longer giddy, and faced the precipice of 3,500 feet without a shiver. Repassing the Ledge and Lift, we accomplished the descent through 1,500 feet of ice and snow, with many falls and bruises, but no worse mishap, and there separated, the young men taking the steepest but most direct way to the "Notch," with the intention of getting ready for the march home, and "Jim" and I taking what he thought the safer route for me—a descent over boulders 2,000 feet, and then a tremendous ascent to the "Notch." I had various falls, and once hung by my frock, which caught on a rock, and "Jim" severed it with his hunting knife, upon which I fell into a crevice full of soft snow. We were driven lower down the mountains than he had intended by impassable tracts of ice, and the ascent was tremendous. For the last 200 feet the boulders were of enormous size, and the steepness fearful. Sometimes I drew myself up on hands and knees, sometimes crawled; sometimes "Jim" pulled me up by my arms or a lariat, and sometimes I stood on his shoulders, or he made steps for me of his feet and hands, but at six we stood on the "Notch" in the splendor of the sinking sun, all color deepening, all peaks glorifying, all shadows purpling, all peril past.

"Jim" had parted with his *brusquerie* when we parted from the students, and was gentle and considerate beyond anything, though I knew that he must be grievously disappointed, both in my courage and strength. Water was an object of earnest desire. My tongue rattled in my mouth, and I could hardly articulate. It is good for one's sympathies to have for once a severe experience of thirst. Truly, there was

Water, water, everywhere,
But not a drop to drink.

Three times its apparent gleam deceived even the mountaineer's practised eye, but we found only a foot of "glare ice." At last, in a deep hole, he succeeded in breaking the ice, and by putting one's arm far down one could scoop up a little water in one's hand, but it was tormentingly insufficient. With great difficulty and much assistance I recrossed the "Lava Beds," was carried to the horse and lifted upon him, and when we reached the camping ground I was lifted off him, and laid on the ground wrapped up in blankets, a humiliating termination of a great exploit. The horses were saddled, and the young men were all ready to start, but "Jim" quietly said, "Now, gentlemen, I want a good night's rest, and we shan't stir from here to-night." I believe they were really glad to have it so, as one of them was quite "finished." I retired to my arbor, wrapped myself in a roll of blankets, and was soon asleep.

When I woke, the moon was high shining through the silvery branches, whitening the bald Peak above, and glittering on the great abyss of snow behind, and pine logs were blazing like a bonfire in the cold still air. My feet were so icy cold that I could not sleep again, and getting some blankets to sit in, and making a roll of them for my back, I sat for two hours by the camp-fire. It was weird and gloriously beautiful. The students were asleep not far off in their blankets with their feet towards the fire. "Ring" lay on one side of me with his fine head on my arm, and his master sat smoking, with the fire lighting up the handsome side of his face, and except for the tones of our voices, and an occasional crackle and splutter as a pine knot blazed up, there was no sound on the mountain side. The beloved stars of my far-off home were overhead, the Plough and Pole Star, with their steady light; the glittering Pleiades, looking larger than I ever saw them, and

"Orion's studded belt" shining gloriously. Once only some wild animals prowled near the camp, when "Ring," with one bound, disappeared from my side; and the horses, which were picketed by the stream, broke their lariats, stampeded, and came rushing wildly towards the fire, and it was fully half an hour before they were caught and quiet was restored. "Jim," or Mr. Nugent, as I always scrupulously called him, told stories of his early youth, and of a great sorrow which had led him to embark on a lawless and desperate life. His voice trembled, and tears rolled down his cheek. Was it semi-conscious acting, I wondered, or was his dark soul really stirred to its depths by the silence, the beauty, and the memories of youth?

We reached Estes Park at noon of the following day. A more successful ascent of the Peak was never made, and I would not now exchange my memories of its perfect beauty and extraordinary sublimity for any other experience of mountaineering in any part of the world. Yesterday snow fell on the summit, and it will be inaccessible for eight months to come.

I.L.B. ✦

About This Story

Isabella Bird was a "tenderfoot"—British writers who would travel the world, and share their accounts of exotic places. Bird was drawn to Colorado where she had heard the air was excellent for the infirm. The vivid letters she sent her sister from the Rocky Mountain region propelled much of the early interest in the area, fueling the growth of the lodging and tourism industries that would later come to define Estes Park. We first heard Bird's descriptions in the welcome film at the Beaver Meadows Visitor Center and immediately sought out her writing.

In this exciting letter, Bird recounts climbing Longs Peak, the tallest in the park. Bird's climb is the first recorded ascent by a woman, which she completed with her rugged guide, "Mountain Jim," an outlaw with one eye and an affinity for both violence and poetry. Though Bird relied heavily on Jim for parts of the ascent and descent, she completed this epic climb wearing only a thin Hawaiian riding dress. The feat speaks to the grit and character that underlay her ability to capture, in beautiful prose, the many places she traveled.

Yellow-Bellied Marmots

SUEELLEN CAMPBELL

I love to think about marmots, to imagine their mountainy lives in subalpine Bower meadows and tundra fellfields, places I can only visit and dream: how in late summer, when gentians bloom deep purple in wet valleys and creamy celadon on high slopes, they eat and laze until they're nearly spherical, savings-account balloons of mitochondria-rich baby fat; how one day in the fall, when ptarmigans are maybe half white, they trundle through cool dim tunnels to nestle in their hibernacula, resting all winter in what biologists call paradoxical sleep, burning some of those fat savings every fortnight or so to rouse from their torpor, nobody knows why, calm and warm, protected by the earth itself, the ground above them blanketed by deep snow or scrubbed by icy gales; how those that survive rise up again in spring, to stretch and stand and greet the sun and meadows and rocks, surely full of joy to be back in the light, breathing the clean, sweet air.

I especially love to imagine them—or better yet, watch them—in summer, when blossoms are bright, nutritious, and abundant: how they tumble about playing and quarreling, babies just weeks old and elders with up to sixteen years on Earth; how the light sparkles and gleams in their fur, chestnuts, golds, and

ivories shimmering like Thai silk, thickly velvet to the
eye's touch; how they roll in and out of rock piles and
holes in the ground, popping up yards from where
they vanished; how they search out dandelions, those
fireworks of solar energy; how they pause and stare
when they see me, wondering whether to hide, relaxing
as I hold still; how they chirp out warnings and say
who knows what else, one-syllable mountain poems
sailing across whole hillsides; and best of all, how they
bask in the warm sun, gazing from rock perches at big
views, across Forest Canyon, for instance, just below the
Ute Trail on an early August afternoon, storm clouds
boiling up, tundra sloping down towards thick dark
woods, glimmering tarns strung upwards through stair-
stepping cirques in the middle distance, and then, above
and beyond to the far horizon, waves of pale shining
granite peaks. ✦

About This Story

Every year, a small fleet of snowplows gear up to clear a path on Trail Ridge Road, 12,183 feet above sea level. Their heroic efforts keep the highest continuous motor road in the United States open each year from roughly late May to late October (at the mercy of weather). Our June visit to the Rockies found us calling the road status line, hoping for a chance to visit the alpine tundra, which makes up one-third of this park. The wait was worth it, as our little Subaru brought us into a dramatic and breathtaking world.

SueEllen Campbell's poem describes one of the few animals designed to survive in the extreme cold, high winds, and intense dryness of the alpine climate: the yellow-bellied marmot. We met one on our drive along Trail Ridge Road, chirping at us from the side of the trail, warning us not to get too close. After we departed, our little marmot friend would spend the rest of its summer gorging and building up body fat to prepare for the eight-month hibernation ahead.

Secret Elk Study Revealed

CURT BUCHHOLTZ

Much to my surprise, upon leaving park headquarters the other day, I walked to my car and discovered an envelope tucked beneath its windshield wipers. Scrawled upon it was the note: "Elk study."

The parking lot was strangely deserted. A short distance away, in the meadow beyond, grazed a half dozen bull elk. I sensed that they eyed me suspiciously while I tore open the envelope.

"We read about your Nature Association and your Park Service!" the scribbling began. "We read about how you caught 50 elk and put radio collars on them. We read about how you plan to count them every year for five years. And we think you're up to no good! We think that after five years you're just going to tell us you've got too many elk!"

"Well, we've got news for you, buddy!" the scribble continued. "There aren't too many elk, Mister Smarty Pants! There are too many people!"

Attached to that note was a fifty page, single spaced report. By its heft alone you could tell someone had compiled a ton of statistics and a pound or two of verbiage. Swiftly, I thumbed through this document, looking for some telltale sign of what it all meant.

My eyes settled on a heading titled "Executive Summary."

"In 1990," it began, "the Elk Study team darted, tranquilized, and collared fifty human beings."

I could hardly believe my eyes. Amazed, I read on.

"Locations for the collaring included Horseshoe Park, Moraine Park, and the Estes Valley Golf Course. Dates of collaring ranged from September 1 through September 30, 1990. The purpose of this study was to trace the movements and conduct a census of humans within Rocky Mountain National Park and the Estes Valley during a five-year period."

"Holy Cats!" I whispered aloud. "How did they do that?"

"Our analysis of human movement prior to the study revealed concentrations of human activity in the Horseshoe Park area during our (previously rather private) rutting season. This influx of humans has made them especially vulnerable to the "stare and snare" capture technique. The largest number (28 or 56%) of individuals were trapped and collared in this location."

"Secondarily, Moraine Park offered significant concentrations along the Cub Lake Trail. Nocturnal trapping activity ranged from the east and southeast grid of Moraine Park Campground. A total of 18 (or 36%) of the captures occurred within this matrix."

"The fewest captures (4 or 8%) occurred on the Estes Park Golf Course. While this human population was older than the average and was the primary target for capturing and collaring, the team discovered that this population was most susceptible to shock and sudden death. Three humans died during the initial phase of our collaring operation and before we realized their susceptibility to stress."

"Success of darting and collaring was largely due to the new generation of tranquilizers now commonly used by the human population. Many of the collared humans, in fact, were approached and successfully captured and collared while dozing."

"The five-year tracking study detailed the movements of these 50 humans and their associated herds. This study enabled us to determine whether their population was increasing or decreasing. It also allowed us to determine their patterns of movement and the extent of their range."

"SUMMARY: After five years, two (2) of the four (4) humans (or 50%) captured on the Estes Valley Golf Course were found in the general area. Captured in 1990 near the 6th green, in 1995, the two remaining were spotted together approaching the 17th tee. We cannot hypothesize about the two missing humans, except to say that our earlier experience with stress among these particular mammals does not bode well for their survival."

"At the Moraine Park location, after five years, only three (or 16.66%) of the original population remained. It is our suspicion that those three may not be among the typical mobile population of humans, but rather part of an indigenous species related somehow to park management. Interestingly, the three were spotted within a quarter mile of their original capture site. We cannot explain the loss of all other subject humans, and cannot attribute their loss to mortality. Instead, it is possible this Moraine Park site hosts a basically transient population."

"At Horseshoe Park, after five years, only one (or 3.57%) of our trapped and collared humans could be found. While this site was densely populated during the capture period—and even more so in 1995—we cannot empirically explain the lack of collared humans. It has been argued in previous studies (Malthus, Erlich) that human populations rise and decline. Yet the human population at Horseshoe Park, in particular, demonstrated increased general density in 1995 as compared to 1990, even though collared humans were absent. We speculate that the 1990 collared humans may have chosen less dense sites if they were visiting in 1995."

"Satellite tracking provided a range study for 31 (62%) of the collared humans. We caution that subject individuals may not represent herd movements. But single individuals were tracked to Japan (#16, #18, #34), Australia (#4), and Germany (#6, #24). A total of six (6) ranged to Denver; five (5) ranged to Fort Collins-Greeley. Surprisingly, fourteen (14) ranged to a single city in Iowa, specifically Des Moines."

"CONCLUSIONS: Our population study reveals the density of humans increasing 28% between 1990 and 1995, or an average increase of 5.8% annually during the month of September.

While the density of humans is increasing, the transient nature of the human population is also evident. Both individuals and—we surmise—herds are far more fickle regarding territoriality than our earlier studies demonstrated (Morris, Gibbon). Within the five-year period, few humans remained in or returned to their original capture sites."

"RECOMMENDATION: Before any radical solution for the culling [of] the human population from the areas in question can be proposed, additional studies should be conducted. A dissenting minority of this study team, however, insists that immediate measures be taken to reduce the human population."

As I finished reading, I looked over my shoulder to see six bull elk stepping closer, as if grazing and glancing at the same time. I jumped in my car and sped away. ✦

About This Story

It was only near the end of our interview that Curt Buchholtz, historian, author, and Director of the National Park Foundation's Intermountain Region, understood the full scope of our project. "You're trying to find a story that you read, and say, 'THAT'S the place.' That's not easy." "Tell us about it," we thought. Curt considered a moment, and asked, "What are you doing next Tuesday?"

Curt took us for an insider tour of his Rocky Mountains, giving us a glimpse in the process as to how hard naturalists, like Curt, fight to protect these spaces. Thanks to his and others' preservation efforts, elk have become one of the iconic attractions of the Rockies. You actually can't get away from them: they're grazing in the park, strolling in the town, and lounging on the golf course. And with no predators, it's the National Park Service that has had to manage their population. With just the right amount of satire, Buchholtz imagines a world in which the elk have their own bureaucracy, for which they write executive summaries, and point out the real population that needs management.

The Legend of the Blue Mist

BILL ROBINSON

The best time to tell this story is on a cloudy overcast evening because that's when these events happened. The whole story takes place in the Fall River Valley.

I've never been able to check as to when Miner Bill, who is the principal character of our story, came into this country. Miner Bill probably followed the Platte River looking for gold, and then caught the Thompson finding a trace of gold there. From there he branched out on Fall River and finally located a mile and a half above Chasm Falls which later became Rocky Mountain National Park. He never acquired any deed to this land or anything. He just built a cabin there, dug a mine and then settled in.

He was a very strange man. I heard that he was the step brother to William Oppenheimer, who was connected with the Manhattan Project. Miner Bill knew enough to understand the tremendous power of what they were creating. That's why he decided to become a hermit up on Old Fall River Road.

There was a lodge up there, the Fall River Lodge (Inn), built around 1908. About 1939, I came into the picture there at the lodge. A friend of mine managed the saddle horses at the lodge, and I came in to run it for him. This is where my first acquaintance with Miner Bill was.

They (the National Park Service) had just opened Trail Ridge Road so I assume it must have been about '33 or '34. (Then) they closed Old Fall River Road down for a good number of years. That is where Miner Bill lived as a hermit. People here in town, Ron Brodie for one, say that Miner Bill would come to town once a year. They would gather him in, make sure he had a bath, clean him up, provision him and then send him back up there.

As I say, in 1939 I became acquainted with Miner Bill because we had a lot of horseback trips up that way. He was very elusive, though. He would hide when you came in sight. But after so many trips up and down he finally came out and made his presence known. He asked if we would pick up provisions for him in town and drop them off. He was very happy, and I'm sure he eked out enough gold from the hill up there to make a living, at least he never wanted for anything.

When he sent us to town in those days it was real strange to carry a little poke of gold dust. You'd have to go to The Estes Park Bank, to Charles Hix down there, and he would weigh it out and give Miner Bill credit in an account he kept down there. You'd buy provisions for him then and take them back up to him.

About, oh, 1941 they reopened the road (Fall River Road) and there was a lot of travel going up and down. Miner Bill would sit out there, and if people saw him they would jump out and take his picture. Well, he thought this was a pretty lucrative thing so he started charging to have his picture taken. If people didn't pay, say if somebody just stopped their car and took his picture, when they'd get up the road around the next switchback he'd fire his old, rusty gun at them and scare the heck out of them. Well, the Park Service didn't go for that and they tried to evict him, but he claimed that he had lived there so long that he had squatter's rights on that land. So, there wasn't much they could do about him.

Things were status quo for probably five or six years from '39 on. At that time there was a young man in Denver, a radio announcer named Troy Torland, who was just breaking into radio. He was one of the first backpackers we ever saw up here. Back in those days you could ride all day in the National Park and not see another soul because the hiker and the backpacker hadn't really come into this area yet. Troy happened to be one of the first ones, and he loved to hike. He didn't care about horses, though. He would ask us to take his provisions on horseback to where he was going, but he'd say that he'd rather walk.

So, he hiked in, and it was late one September that Troy came into the lodge. He'd always leave his car at the garage, and he'd say, "I'll be back tomorrow," or "I'll be back two days from now." So we knew when to start looking if he didn't show up. He was a real responsible young man though. So, he left on this late September day and shortly after one of these early winter storms with the clouds came in. A lot of you have probably been up here when the clouds seem to settle right in the whole valley and just cover everything. Well, this was one of those storms.

Troy had gone up the old Ute Trail and cut down by Iceberg Lake down to Willow Park and was coming out the Old Fall River Road when the clouds just really closed in. The only way he could find his way back down was by following the sound of the river.

All of a sudden Troy said he saw a light, and so he made his way to the light, which happened to be this old cabin that Miner Bill had built. This cabin, incidentally, had eight sides on it. Miner Bill had built it out of logs. It had a real pointed roof and a big flat rock on the roof. Whenever somebody asked Miner Bill what the rock was for, he'd say that it was to ward off the evil spirits. Really it was to keep the wind from blowing the roof off in the winter.

Troy went up and knocked on the door. Miner Bill came to the door, and Troy told him that the weather had closed him out. He was seeking shelter for a little bit until he could get his bearings. Miner Bill said, "Well, I was about ready to eat, and I've got plenty for you. So, why don't you come in and have dinner."

So, Troy went in and ate dinner, and they started talking and found they had a lot of mutual interests. Troy loved the outdoors and Miner Bill did, too. Troy knew enough about his past or people he had been with so they talked until probably three or four o'clock in the morning. Troy got in the next day, and told us he had spent the night with Miner Bill which seemed real unusual to us. He said, "He's a nice old man, and we have a lot of common interests. I'm goin' to come back every chance I get, and go up and see him." He did this for about two years. Every free weekend he had Troy went up and saw Miner Bill, and he'd spend the night with him. So, knowing Troy, we got a little more acquainted with Miner Bill and probably did a few more favors for him and what not.

Well, World War II came along about that time. Troy went into the service. Shortly after I went in. Two years later I was back on furlough. Troy happened to be here at the same time on furlough, so he went up to see Miner Bill, and I rode the country. When Troy got back he said, "Something is happenin' up there. I don't know what it is, but Miner Bill is real nervous about whatever it is."

So, we left that summer and came back a year and a half later. I beat Troy back out, and the first thing I did was come up to the lodge. It was late fall, and so I rode a few of the trails. I looked the country over and happened to stop by to see Miner Bill. He was real elusive, and I thought, well, I've been away for a couple of years. He doesn't remember me and what not. But after talking to him it didn't bridge a gap in there, and I knew there was something wrong.

It was the next spring before Troy came back, and he came in the lodge early that spring. He said, "I've got to go up and see Miner Bill." So, he went up and came back a couple of days later. He brought us a list of provisions that Miner Bill needed. He said, "The first chance you get, you take these to him and check on him. I'll be back up. I'm not going to go back to my job right away. I'm going to come up and spend two or three weeks with him. I'll try to talk him into leaving the hills and going back to Denver with me."

Well, the next day I took the provisions up to Miner Bill, and there was funny feeling about the whole area up there. I think Miner Bill probably tried to give us this impression, but there was something strange. So, about a week later Troy came up, and he said, "I'm going in for a couple of weeks to hike and spend some time with Miner Bill." So, he went up there. Probably a week later I rode by and I didn't see anyone. I heard a dog barking which was real strange because Miner Bill didn't keep pets around. He had a few chickens out in the chicken house to furnish him eggs and meat but that was about all. He ran a little trap line 'cause there were a lot of deer and elk up there.

Well, I heard this dog barking. So, I went over and tied my horse and looked in the cabin window. There was a big Doberman pinscher dog chained up in the cabin. There was one post right in the middle of the cabin holding the roof up that this dog was chained to it. I thought this was a little strange. There was no sign of either Troy or Bill, so I went back to the lodge.

It was probably about four or five days later that Troy came back to the lodge. He said, "Something is happening up at Miner Bill's in that particular area that I'm not familiar with. I can't get any information out of Miner Bill at all, but something is developing there that only he is aware of."

Troy said that he had two or three job interviews. He'd be gone for about a month, but would be back at the end of August. He wanted to go up there then and bring Miner Bill out.

In the intervening time we'd drive by there to check on him. Miner Bill would generally leave a little note on the door if he needed anything, provisions or what not and the few letters he got. He got quite a few letters, actually, for being a hermit, and a lot of scientific journals and what not came in. We'd generally pick up his mail, which was delivered to the lodge, and anybody going by would just drop it off. He had credit at the Bank to buy his provisions. Probably three times the next month he left messages on the door for supplies of one sort or another, and we'd pick them up and deliver them.

Troy came back that August and went up there and spent three days. He came back and said, "I can't talk the old man into coming out, he's going to stay there. But something is wrong up there, I know it. I've got a job in New York, and I'll be gone about three months. But I'll be back, and we'll try it again."

At that time I was goin' to school down in Fort Collins, but I spent all my weekends up at the lodge. So, it was late in December that I happened to be up there on the weekend. We'd had a kind of nasty weather situation that month, and there was probably a foot and a half of snow on the ground up there.

Troy pulled in late Friday evening and said, "I'll spend the night with you all here. The first thing in the morning I'm going up, and I'm going to talk Miner Bill into coming out. He just can't survive another winter up there."

So, Troy went up, and the clouds really came in. We had probably four or five inches of fresh snow before the storm quit, but then the clouds settled back into the valley. Monday passed and Tuesday passed, and the clouds hadn't lifted. Early on Wednesday morning Troy came back down. He came in about breakfast time, which means that he'd had to have left there about midnight to have made his way down.

Troy sat down and had breakfast with us. He never said a word. We all finished breakfast and started to make plans for the day, going this way and that way. Finally he said, "I've just got to talk to somebody, and we've got to do something with Miner Bill. We went through an experience this weekend that you wouldn't believe." We said, "So all right, let's have it."

Troy said that he got up there and settled in, but Miner Bill wouldn't hardly talk to him for the first day he was there. He spent the night, and this would have been probably on a Sunday or Monday. He said that they'd just finished dinner and were going to bed when the dog started growling. Troy said, "This was the first time I'd ever heard that dog make a sound at night when we're all locked up there. With that growling and all, Miner Bill just went into a rage. He went from one side of the cabin to the other and kept looking out the window."

Troy said it was pitch black and snowing with the clouds on the ground. He didn't think there was anything out there. He thought probably a bear came down or something. Well, the dog finally settled down. Troy got hold of Miner Bill and sat him down and asked, "What is going on up here?" Miner Bill said, "I don't know what is going on up here, but whatever it is has been haunting me for the last six years. Come here and I'll show you." He grabbed his old oil lantern, and went out in the snow.

Around the cabin there were some real big Englemann spruce trees, probably stood eighty or ninety feet tall. There were no limbs until you got up to thirty feet. Miner Bill shone the light up on these trees. Troy said, "I don't know what he was lookin' at on the bark of those trees." Miner Bill said to Troy, "Little higher, little higher." Troy kept looking up, and finally he could see some marks on the trees. He said, "Yea, there's some marks on the trees up there. A bear probably climbed up there." Miner Bill said, "No, no that isn't a bear. You wait, you wait until morning. We'll come out in the daylight, and I'll show you what it is."

Well, they got back in the cabin and almost settled in when the dog started growling again. This time he was lunging against his chain in the middle of the floor. Troy got up, and he looked up the canyon toward Iceberg Lake where that gorge comes down. He said, "There was a blue light kind of shining. It must have been a reflection of something coming off of something else. This blue haze kept shifting down, and as it got closer, the dog growled more. Pretty soon this light came right into the cabin area. I've never seen anything like it before. It was like a mist in the clouds. It settled into a tree out there just like it was hanging onto the tree or surrounding it."

"Miner Bill was just completely erratic. He was just going from room to room, and the dog was making such a fuss and what not. All of a sudden the light was gone, and the dog settled right down on the floor. Miner Bill just went to bed and never said another word. I stayed up the rest of the night looking out the window. Dawn came and we went outside. There was probably four or five inches of fresh snow on the ground on top of the foot and a half to two feet that was already there. There was not one animal track in that whole area, not even a rabbit track."

He said he looked up at this tree that this blue haze had evidently been around. There was a three-toed claw mark about twenty feet up on the tree. He said he got to looking around, and every tree but one around that whole place had a three-toed mark on it.

Troy said there was no explanation that he knew of. He walked over to the tree where there were bark peelings on the ground, right in the fresh snow. There wasn't a track up to it. He said, "There surely must be a bear that flies up there. I can't explain it, but I'm going to get out of here." The day after that, when the weather broke, Troy told Miner Bill, "In two weeks I'm going to come back up here, and I'm going to get you out of here." Miner Bill said, "Well, whatever."

So, that's the story Troy related to us. Curiosity got the best of us by then. Two days later there was a bright, beautiful, sunny day, and we saddled up some horses and rode up there. We plunged our way up through the snow, and got up there and sure 'nough on those trees were the marks. Some of them looked like they were six or seven years old. We thought that maybe old Miner Bill had been crawling up the tree with a knife and carving these marks in it, but they really didn't look that way. It looked like an animal had put the marks in the trees. As a matter of fact, those marks are still visible up there in those trees. They're well overgrown and scarred over, but you can still see where these marks are in the trees. Anyway, when we went up there we saw that right in front of the main door of the cabin there was one tree that didn't have a mark on it.

Two weeks later Troy came up. The weather was nasty that winter like the last two winters we've had, it was bad. Troy went up one day and came back that night. He said, "Miner Bill isn't goin' to move. I've got to go to Kansas City. I'll be gone about three weeks, and then I'll be back."

Well, this put it into the first part of February when Troy rolled in late one Friday evening. He said, "I'll go up and pack everything that Miner Bill has, and leave it packed. In the spring when you get up there with horses you bring it out, but I'm going to bring Bill out with me."

So, he left early Saturday morning and said, "I'll be out probably tomorrow, but if the weather closes in, we'll be out whenever it breaks." Well, we had another storm come in. It was one of those funny storms again where the clouds come down, not too much snow and not too much wind. The clouds just settled back down on the ground. So, it was late Tuesday evening, and we were starting to wonder what had happened to Troy and Miner Bill.

I'd gone back to school, and I drove back every night from Fort Collins just to see if Troy had come back. I got back up there about eight-thirty that night and Troy hadn't come out. I decided to stay over, and Wednesday morning we were going to go up and find them. We all went to bed that night, and it must have been about one-thirty or two o'clock in the morning when the clouds lifted a little bit, and the wind started blowing. It was drifting the snow pretty badly. The wind probably woke me up.

I was laying there at probably one-thirty in the morning when I heard some-body banging on the front door of the lodge. I was up on the second floor so the owner of the lodge got there before I did. He opened the door, and there stood Troy. Troy said, "We've got to get to town. We've got to get Miner Bill to town." We said, "Fine, we've got the old Ford truck chained up, and I think we can make it into town." We asked what happened. Troy said, "His head is caved in." With that we gathered up a lot of tarps and quilts. Troy had brought Miner Bill out by lashing three skis together and tying Bill to them. Well, we just picked up Miner Bill, skis and all, and loaded him in the back of the old truck.

Old Doc Mall was practicing then. We got him out of bed, and he met us down at the clinic. After looking at Miner Bill, Doc Mall said, "There isn't too much I can do for him here." He told us to get him to Greeley about as quick as we could. If we did, there might be a chance to save the old man.

We headed right off to Greeley and arrived at the hospital an hour and a half later. They took him right in. Troy told us to go back up, and he would stay down there until Bill was out of danger.

Late Wednesday evening Troy came back up. We asked him what had happened. He said, "You're not going to believe this story. I had him convinced to leave when the clouds came in. We were puttering around the kitchen packing up his utensils and personal belongings. All of a sudden the dog started growling, and I looked out of the window. There was that blue light again. It just seemed to hover around. One time it went clear up to the needles on Ypsilon Mountain. It sat up there for an hour. All of a sudden it came back down and lit in this one tree that didn't have the claw marks in it."

"Miner Bill lost his mind. He grabbed his old rusty gun from above the door. As he opened the door, the Doberman lunged and broke his chain and ran out. The dog leaped up the tree, and just as soon as he jumped he was laying in the doorway. The dog's throat was cut. With that, Miner Bill ran out and started shooting that old lever action gun up in the tree. Soon as he got under the tree a branch must have broken and hit him in the head. When Bill hit the ground, it was dark out there, no blue mist or anything. I assume that one of his shells hit an old limb and weakened it."

Miner Bill lived, but his mind was not quite right from that day on. They put him down in the State home. Every once in a while he'd slip away from them, and three or four days later they'd go pick him up at his old cabin.

At that time our District Ranger was named Lauren Lane. He and I did a lot of plowing around up there. We took casts of these supposed claw marks. We took pictures, but nothing ever came of it. We thought Miner Bill was just an old man who got hit on the head with a tree branch.

About three years went by, and a group from the Fort Collins Ski Club came up. They were going to Lawn Lake on an overnight. They skied up there on a beautiful moonlit night. They were all full of energy, and they decided to ski up to Crystal before goin' to bed. So, about eighteen of them hiked the trail up to Crystal Lake. One by one they came back down. It was so light that you could see everyone on the hill.

Everybody came down, but the last person decided to go up to Rowe Glacier which was probably a hundred and fifty yards. They could see him walking up there for most of the way, but then he disappeared around the bend for just a minute. Just then a blue haze rose up from Crystal Lake. They said they could see him and then they couldn't. They sat there and waited and waited, but he didn't come down. They waited an hour. Three of the party decided to go up there. They could see where they had come down. They could see where their companion had telemarked up the hill and turned, but that was it. His tracks just stopped right there. They made big circles around and couldn't find a trace of him. They sent two boys down.

These boys arrived at the lodge about four-thirty in the morning. We called Lauren Lane, and he organized a search party. In those days there were probably ten personnel in Rocky Mountain National Park in the winter. We headed up about eight-thirty that morning and got up there about noon. We found the tracks but no trace of the skier—nothing, nothing. Off to the right about ten feet from his track were these three tracks coming down the mountain. The body was never found. We all figured when the snow melted off in the spring somebody would stumble across the body.

Nothing happened for four years. Then, ironically, there was another group from Fort Collins, a hiking group. They were going over Flattop Mountain, spending the night along the trail and then being picked up in Grand Lake. They started off and sure enough the clouds settled in. It was a nasty fall day.

One of the party, a boy from New Jersey, had a touch of mountain sickness. They were sitting around on a bunch of scattered rocks when the clouds came in. The clouds were so heavy that they couldn't see each other. Pretty soon they noticed kind of a blue tinge in the clouds like the sun or moon was trying to break through the clouds. This blue haze moved right down through the middle of them.

About twenty minutes later the clouds lifted, and the boy that wasn't feeling good was gone. They thought that he had started back down the trail, so four of the group went back down to Bear Lake. They didn't find their friend, so they notified the Park Rangers. The search party didn't find a trace of the boy except where he was sitting there was this same three claw marks.

This boy's folks came out here for probably ten years. By that time I was working at Stead's Ranch, and they stayed there because it was the closest place. They would spend their time up on Flattop looking for their boy. But there again, fact or fiction, everybody saw the blue cloud and the three marks.

The next year, late in the fall, we had one of those sudden storms. It caught a lot of people in Grand Lake that wanted to come back over. Lauren called me and said that they were going to form a convoy and send these people over from Grand Lake. He wanted to know if I wanted to ride along. I was trying to close up the lodge for the winter, so I didn't go.

They went over, and there were probably twenty cars at Grand Lake that they convoyed back. They would open the gates, and the last Ranger through would close and lock the gate. The last car was a station wagon with three young children in it. They had just come over the top, and right before the Iceberg Lake turnout one of the children got a little carsick.

The folks in the station wagon happened to notice a blue mist rising up out of Iceberg Lake. The Ranger following behind locking the gates saw the car pull over, so he turned on his red lights. Well, by that time the boy was feeling better, so the folks pulled back on the road. The Ranger was familiar with the legend, so he stopped where the car had been. He could see where they had stopped because the heat of the tires had melted the snow. He said that right beside where the car was sitting was that three-toed claw mark in the snow. He came on down and called me and asked if I wanted to see the marks. We went right back up there, and sure enough there they were.

So, everything settled down, and there wasn't a sign until five years ago. There were a couple of kids out from Minneapolis. They were going to try to ski in to Chasm Lake, but they only got to Jim's Grove. It was a bad night. They weren't used to the altitude so hypothermia set in. The girl had injured herself so the young man left her in a sleeping bag and went for help. When they didn't show up at the appointed time, the Park Service organized a search party. They went into Jim's Grove and found her and brought her out. They searched for him off and on for three months before the search was given up. There wasn't a sign of him.

The next incident was probably the third or fourth of May that year. We had a real nasty night. It was kind of in between snow and rain. There was a car driving up the south St. Vrain. They came around a curve, and there was this beautiful blue light up there. They thought it was one of the strangest things they had ever seen. They drove on into Estes and were sitting in one of the restaurants in town. They happened to mention to their waitress about the strange blue light. She was an old timer and had heard the story of the blue mist, and so she mentioned it around. Well, the Sheriff's Department was notified. They went out to investigate and probably fifty yards off the road, they found that young boy who had died of hypothermia probably three months before. Where he was found was the focal point of where the blue light had been.

Well, that was the end of the story until last winter. A group of hikers were going to scale Mt. Lady Washington, coming over from Grand Lake. They were all very experienced mountain climbers. They got up within about fifty yards of the summit, and that was as close as they could get. The wind came up and drove the chill factor down to probably sixty below. They decided to turn around.

There was a young lady from Longmont in the party who decided to go on. When they got back to their base camp she didn't show up. The Park Service was notified the next morning. They went in from the Thunder Lake side. On that particular day the wind was fierce, and the wind chill was still fifty or sixty below zero. She had bright orange clothing on, and as they crossed over the saddle above the lake, she stood out on the hillside. One of the men with the search party said that it was the strangest thing when they got to her because the wind had obliterated all tracks around her except three marks in the snow.

That ends the legend right there. Fact or fiction, I don't know. I've never seen the blue mist, but I've seen the evidence. Who knows if it's happenstance or what. During the winter you get all sorts of strange things happening, and the clouds play funny tricks in the summer ... ✦

About This Story

The YMCA of the Rockies and Cheley Colorado Camps established facilities in the park to use the outdoors as a teaching tool for youth. One famous story says that, after staying at the YMCA of the Rockies' outdoor facilities, W. C. Coleman decided to manufacture camping gear.

While we weren't looking for spooky stories, "The Blue Mist" is too good not to share. "The Blue Mist" tells the story of a hermit who finds refuge in the mountains, but is haunted by the quick-changing mountain weather. A sunny day gives way to a windy thunderstorm. A clear afternoon turns into a hazy mist. During our stay, we encountered light rainfall every day, only to have it clear up by afternoon. The mountains create their own weather, they say, but it's easy to imagine that the mist could be carrying something else.

Excerpt from
"Children of My Trail School"

ENOS MILLS

One summer day nearly twenty years ago a number of boys and girls appeared at my Rocky Mountain cabin. They wanted me to go with them to the old beaver colony. A boy and a girl started making the request, but before they could finish every child was asking me to go. "It is more than two miles," I told them, "and we must walk." This but added to their desire to go at once.

Stepping softly and without saying a word, we slipped through the woods and peeped from behind the last trees into a grassy opening by the beaver pond, hoping for a glimpse of a coyote or a deer. Then we examined the stumps of aspens recently cut by the beavers. We walked across the dam. We made a little raft of logs and went out to the island house in the pond. Then we built tiny beaver houses and also dugouts in the bank. We played we were beavers.

On the way home we turned aside from the trail to investigate a delightful bit of forested wilderness between two brooks. We were explorers in a new country. The grove was dense and full of underbrush. It was voted to send out a likely boy and girl to discover how many hundred miles it was through the forest. While waiting we decided to examine one of the brooks, which someone called the Amazon River. We found a delta which one boy insisted was the delta at the mouth of the Mississippi. No one objected and we had discussions concerning deltas, large and small. But the vast wilderness between our two brooks—which contained really about one acre—was reported by our two scouts as altogether too large for us ever to explore.

Someone then proposed we should cross the brook on a fallen log to see who the strange people were in the wilderness on the other side. The last boy of the party made a long jump from the end of the log and declared he had jumped across a nation—that one boundary line was the end of the log and the other was where he alighted. Just where the remaining two lines should be provoked a profound discussion, as boundary lines of nations often do. It was finally agreed that the other lines should be determined by one of the girls taking a hop, skip and jump.

We decided to take a census and at once everyone began to count the inhabitants of this nation. We found a number of bugs, spiders, and beetles; then other beetles and a few grasshoppers; and finally everyone surrounded a swarming ant hill, trying to determine how to make an accurate count of this warlike and numerous tribe. This was never settled, for suddenly a big grasshopper with black and yellow wings entered the nation from the outside. He alighted for only a moment and then flew away again. The opinion was about equally divided as to whether he should be counted as one of the inhabitants or an invader.

At this stage someone broke the news that it was already too late for us to reach home for lunch. So intense had been the interest that we had forgotten even to keep track of mealtime. Two likely boys were sent out to forage for rations, with suggestions that they go to the kitchen and procure supplies enough to prevent starvation among the explorers until night, and return by the shortest route.

While we were eating merrily round a camp-fire by the brook a wasp and a fly engaged in a struggle on a mountainside. The top of the mountain was no higher than the knee of the boy who stood by it. When this life and death struggle ended by the contestant falling over a precipice thousands of feet below, everyone concluded it was time to go home.

That evening these excited and enthusiastic boys and girls related the day's experience to any one who would listen. They had been explorers in a wilderness, had camped by mighty rivers, had seen wild animals and strange nations. Their imaginations were on fire. This world has become an inexhaustible wonderland.

These children were dealing with real things through interest, and their imaginations blazed with more keenness than it was possible for the powers of legends and fairytales to incite. They had been to school, had studied, had worked, had learned without realizing it. Their reports amounted to enthusiastic recitations of new, big lessons well learned. Best of all, they were happy, and were eager to go on with this schooling—this developing. We have continued these excursions somewhat irregularly through the years to the present time and handled them with increasing effectiveness.

While a guide on Long's Peak I developed what may be called the poetic interpretation of the facts of nature. Scientific names in a dead language together with classifications that dulled interest were ever received, as they should have been, with indifference and lack of enthusiasm by those who did not know. Hence I began to state information about most things in the form of its manners and customs, its neighbours and its biography.

Nature's storybook is everywhere and always open. And I wish children might have everywhere what the children have had here in enjoyment, educational foundation, and incentive. What we are doing here may be done elsewhere.

John Muir, in writing his boyhood experiences, says: "The animals about us were a never-ending source of wonder and delight. How utterly happy it made us! Nature streaming into us, wooingly teaching her wonderful, glowing lessons so unlike the dismal, grim ashes and cinders so long thrashed into us. Here, without knowing it, we still were in school; every wild lesson a love lesson, not whipped but charmed into us."

Interest gives the ability and energy to see accurately and the incentive to watch for things that may happen around us; adds purpose to every outdoor day. Such happy experiences based on interest truly enrich life. . . . Interest is the master teacher.

The Robinson Crusoe School was the name someone early applied to us, but later the name Trail School was taken. This school—the great outdoors—is in session whenever children wander over the trail, free from academic chaperonage. The trail supplies materials and equipment, and Mother Nature is an endless mental stimulus.

Most people think that the wilderness is a supremely dangerous place for human beings. They carry through life a handicap of fear of the outdoors. These children learn that the wilds are not only friendly but hospitable; they find ferocious animals only in storybooks, and ere long being out after dark or in the rain is fun. ✦

About This Story

The natural world speaks to anyone of any age, but holds its greatest rewards for those who approach it with childlike wonder and curiosity. In this story by Enos Mills, the famous naturalist follows the lead of a group of children, allowing them to explore and discover, as the lessons of nature take hold.

Enos Mills is remembered as the "Father of Rocky Mountain National Park." Contemporary historians are widening that lens to recognize the advocacy efforts of additional groups, like the Colorado Mountain Club and the Estes Park Woman's Club. But Mills's lectures on behalf of the park idea remain an important part of the story of preserving this stretch of the Rocky Mountains.

According to park ranger Kathy Brazelton, Mills was the first to outline the principles of park interpretation, and one of the first to hire female outdoor guides. In "Children of My Trail School," he outlines some of his ideas that were radical for his time: his empathy for different ways of learning, and his deep appreciation for the natural world as classroom and teacher.

Other Campfires:
Ancient Walls on Trail Ridge

JACK C. MOOMAW

Out of the thousands who annually pass over the Trail Ridge road, perhaps few people give a thought to those of long ago who used practically the same route to cross over the Continental Divide.

Before the automobile road was built, guides, tourists, and rangers, on foot and by horse, followed the trail that wound across the uplands; the hunters and prospectors had passed this way before them, following a trail left by the mountain men and Indians, who in turn had followed a trail that was already old, made hundreds, possibly thousands, of years ago by game and by the feet of men we know very little about. The Indians had a saying which translated means, "Other campfires have burned here before."

One day I found some small automobile parts beside the highway. On the trail I found a rusty horseshoe. A couple of years ago I found an old pinfire cartridge. (Such ammunition was used before the memory of the present generation.) Along the trail I have found flint arrowheads, very likely Ute or Arapahoe; and in a little gravel spot on a bare hilltop far above timberline, parts of Yuma projectile points. Men who have made a study of such things say that Yuma points date back to and before the last ice age.

While standing on that hilltop, trying to picture in my mind a pageant of the type of life that had once traveled through the little pass below, I noticed a line of rocks running down either side of the slope and at right angles to the pass. Now tepee rings are fairly common in the Rockies, but here was something different. The more I looked the plainer the line became, winding this way and that to utilize large boulders. Without a doubt it was the remains of an old wall, almost obliterated in places. I could not help wondering what many of our present walls would look like if left to the elements for a thousand years. These rocks had not been moved in ages, many were embedded in the sod, and all were covered with lichen.

For several weeks I pondered the origin of this line of rocks, and one day with Dean Kirby, Estes Park newspaper man, went back to look at it, when he noticed a second old wall running parallel to the pass, and about one hundred and fifty feet north, and at right angles to the one that I had found. Later I went back to the walls with compass and tape line, and took data, which is rather lengthy and would be out of place in this book.

The total length of both walls is seven hundred and fifty feet. It must have taken considerable effort to build them, and naturally the thought arises, What was the purpose? My first thought was of a fortification, and yet it hardly seems possible that men who lived in that remote time, men whose very lives depended upon constant vigilance, would not have seen, miles away, something suspicious in such walls. A large party of Indians (or mountain men) may have met another large hostile party here and hastily fortified themselves, but roving bands of such men usually knew what possible danger was on the other sides of mountains before they crossed over.

My second thought was that it might be some sort of a game trap, but there are several places on Trail Ridge that seem to me much better fitted for such a purpose, and the absence of arrowheads and broken points argues against it. Over a period of several years, and after going over the ground again, I have found only four arrowheads in the vicinity of the walls.

Ceremonial purposes? Possibly. Who knows what the minds of men in that dim past may have tried to express in strange ceremonies on the high rocky barrens above timberline, surrounded by a vast sea of hills and canyons.

Some day we may find a clue that will lead to the secret, but at present only one thing is certain, "Other campfires have burned here before." ✦

About This Story

Jack Moomaw began guiding tourists through the Rockies in 1915 to supplement his farming income. By 1921, Moomaw was hired as one of the first park rangers, responsible for surveying miles and miles of the early hiking and horse trails in the park.

In each park we visited, we sought native stories by native storytellers, preferring stories that are freed from colonial influence and are told in a tribe member's own words. But in the Rockies, contemporary Ute and Arapaho tribes are less connected to the park than in other places we visited. What's known is that Ute tribes followed animal herds across the tundra roughly 6,000 years ago. Later migrations brought the Apache to the area in the 1500s, and the Arapaho around 1800. These tribes were migratory, and expelled during the early period of US western expansion. Today's park bears many tribal names due to a pack trip in 1914, organized by Harriet Vaille and Edna Hendrie of the Colorado Mountain Club, and documented by Oliver Toll in his book, *Arapaho Names and Trails*. Sadly, this is the extent of the written record.

Instead of reprinting a questionable native story, we're acknowledging that, like Moomaw, we are left wondering about the legacy of those that came before us.

The Mountains Rise

EDNA DAVIS ROMIG

Beyond the forests the mountains rise
    In range on range
so that these fields are lower step
of an ascending stairs
That climb to the blue mountain skies
Through grass and elm and conifer
And granite of eonic change.
The far scene wears
Peace like a coronet.
It has a voice of majesty and wonder . . .
Within those ramparts are
Chasm and precipice
And the thousand thunders
Of waterfall and glacial ice.
Canyons that yawn to black and unknown depth,
Lakes bottomless and cold.
Ledges may be the funeral pyre of planes.
Trails often prove to be the lethal paths
That lead, flower-grown, to death,
And lonely peaks the finger beckoning
To doom.
But the wise climber knows the science of mountains,
And, being the lover,

Pushes on past morraine,
Past col, crag, dome, and snowy fold
To discover
The sun-warmed stone, the tundra, and the Alpine bloom—
At last achieves
The summit. ✦

About This Story

Iconic images of the Rocky Mountains often boast jagged peaks capped with snow. Trail Ridge Road required engineering miracles to lay asphalt at such extreme elevations, and remains a logistical challenge to maintain. But access to these subalpine and alpine ecosystems is what makes a trip to Rocky Mountain National Park so unique.

Romig's visual and lyrical poem evokes many of the natural elements unique to these mountains. The forests that go up and up until one is in the blue mountain sky. The climbers that see those peaks as a challenge, and test their mettle on forlorn ascents. Colorado is full of 14ers, mountain peaks with an elevation of at least 14,000 feet, and Romig's poem sees the mountain as the climber experiences it.

ZION NATIONAL PARK

A Sanctuary in the Desert

NAMED FOR ITS ROLE as a "sanctuary"
and known for its dramatic high sandstone
peaks and narrow slot canyons—Zion
National Park is perhaps less well known
for the "floods and fury" that can be brought
to this lush desert canyon by the very river
that carved it, the Virgin River.

illustration by
MAGGIE CHIANG

Zion National Park was our most difficult park to date. Neither of us had experienced the desert before, and the endless red rock cliffs seemed to intensify the heat as it escalated to 102, 104, 109 degrees Fahrenheit during a mid-June heat wave. If the desert is an acquired taste, we were slow to drink it in.

Most of the wildlife in Zion National Park is nocturnal. And, after just one week of camping in the park, we too adopted the ways of the lizard—lying low in the afternoon and moving around at dawn and at dusk, away from the sun's debilitating grasp. We even swallowed our pride, investing in extreme-weather gear, and our hydration packs became necessary to our survival. The only relief came at night, after 10 p.m., when winds would whip through the canyon. During the day, the heated air rises up through the straight up-and-down shape of Zion Canyon to the plateau. At night, that air cools and blows back down through the canyon—they say this canyon "breathes."

It was here that our research process became even more vital. As we struggled physically to connect to the Utah desert, it was conversations with the rangers and residents that enabled us to see its beauty—many were moved to tears when responding to our question, "What do you love about this place?" Their love and enthusiasm opened our eyes to the beauty of this lush and generous desert.

The name "Zion" was first uttered by Isaac Behunin, one of the original Mormon settlers in the canyon. He said, "A man can worship God among these great cathedrals as well as in any man-made church—this is Zion." Think of Isaac's point of view. Here, the spring-fed Virgin River flowed, giving life to flora and fauna unseen in many desert lands. And for the Mormon people, forced out west to escape religious persecution, the canyon walls, rising 2,000 feet on all sides, offered a sense of peace, and of protection. To these weary travelers, this place must truly have felt like their promised land. To this day, Zion retains its spiritual metaphors. The park celebrated its own centennial in 2009 as "A Century of Sanctuary."

Before it was Zion, famed explorer John Wesley Powell recorded the name Mukuntuweap, as he heard it described by the native Paiute people. Mukuntuweap has been translated as "straight river," "sacred cliffs," and also "straight arrow." Although President Taft declared it Mukuntuweap National Monument in 1909, it was renamed Zion when it became a national park in 1919. Unlike Denali in

Alaska, there is, to date, no movement to return the area to its native name. Given the contested translations of "Mukuntuweap," it's the name Zion that's stuck.

Humans aren't the only species who see the canyon as a sanctuary. Over five hundred times more species are found near the water in the canyon than in the surrounding desert landscape. Zion is home to peregrine falcons, mountain lions, kangaroo rats, and bighorn sheep—all adapted to live in a landscape of cracks, crevices, and cliffs. The Zion snail, for instance, lives only in gardens like the one found at Weeping Rock: a unique ecosystem that clings to the cliff face, supplied by water seeping out the sides of canyon walls. During our visit, endangered California condors were nesting in the park, though tragedy struck just weeks later when one of the pair died after ingesting lead bullets, jeopardizing the future of the rest of the family.

Calling Zion a sanctuary highlights the generosity of the desert, but can mask the fury it holds as well. Rocks still fall from the cliffs as they erode. Flash floods arrive without warning. And the intense heat of the desert challenges the humans who live here. Thank goodness for the Virgin River. Some think that Zion should be called "Virgin River National Park," for it's the river that carved the canyon, brought the settlers, and makes any life here possible. Although a small river, it moves at an extraordinary speed, averaging 60 cubic feet per second. And even when there are blue skies in Zion, rainfall to the north can result in furious flash floods through the canyon, increasing the water flow by up to 2,000 cubic feet per second, bringing whole trees and other debris along with it. In 1995, a massive landslide and flood wiped out the main road, stranding visitors at the Zion Lodge for a few extra nights. In 2015, seven hikers ignored officials' warnings, heading out for a hike under sunny blue skies, and were killed by a flash flood in Keyhole Canyon. The unpredictability of Zion made life difficult for early settlers. Taming the land and growing crops was frequently disrupted when floods, without warning, reconfigured the landscape in an instant. Throughout the park, there are numerous blind arches, remnants of giant boulders that broke free from the canyon wall after water in various rock layers froze and then thawed, eventually sending massive boulders down to the canyon below. One unofficial account tells of a Mormon family returning from Sunday church service to find fragments of a boulder where their farm used to be.

Methodist minister and explorer, Frederick Vining Fisher, came here in 1916 on a trip to name many of the great features of Zion. Fisher declared the tallest mountain the Great White Throne, a seat fit for God, and its shorter neighbor as Angels Landing. Seeing three peaks together, he thought these could only be Abraham, Isaac, and Jacob: the Court of the Patriarchs. These names reflect the history of the Mormon faith, but the Temple of Sinawava recalls the history of Paiute spirituality. Sinawava is Coyote, the hero of many native myths, a mischievous trickster who is also a teacher of people.

Zion is kind of like a geologist's candy store, and they flock here in droves to study and share their joy in these formations. As a park ranger told us, "This is the place where the earth opens itself up and says, 'Here's my story.'" Another spelled out the recipe for the canyon's formation. Step 1: Collect sand, gravel, and mud in a nearly flat basin. Repeat the process of sedimentation until ten thousand feet of material has collected. Step 2: Allow water to seep in, carrying iron oxide, calcium carbonate, and silica to bind all agents, so that, with pressure, sand dunes turn into sandstone. Step 3: Lift area above sea level. Step 4: Unleash the Virgin River, concentrating its mighty flow over the sandstone, eroding it over time to form the canyons and valleys that define this landscape. Millions of years later, enjoy one Zion National Park.

The time it took to create these mountains makes some feel appropriately small. For others, the park may feel more like Disneyworld, as a visit to Zion, during peak months of the year, includes a mandatory shuttle for visitors not travelling to their destination by foot. After experiencing substantial traffic and resource damage, Zion unveiled their shuttle system in 1997 as an alternative to automobiles on the main scenic road. Today, all visitors take shuttles through the nearby town of Springdale enroute to Zion Canyon. Plan to arrive at dawn unless you prefer to wait in long lines in the sweltering sun with hundreds of other visitors for nearly an hour. But it wasn't always this way.

With its tough terrain and limited resources, Zion required a huge marketing effort to attract the general public. The Union Pacific Railroad was an early advocate of this park and key to its eventual popularity and accessibility. Before visitors like us had Subaru Foresters to whip them around the country, the railroads established lines out to the parks, and produced brochures to draw passengers west. They also built grand lodges in Zion and Bryce Canyon, assuring visitors of comfortable accommodations. The Grand Circle tour they created and promoted took visitors by train to Cedar City, Utah, then by bus to Zion National Park, the North Rim at Grand Canyon National Park, Bryce Canyon National Park, and then Cedar Breaks National Monument. Artists also played a vital role in this campaign. As part of John Wesley Powell's 1903 expedition, Frederick S. Dellenbaugh spent much of the summer painting Zion Canyon. His paintings at the St. Louis World's Fair in 1904 and article in *Scribner's Magazine* flowed with superlatives describing Zion's wondrous landscape. Artists like Howard Russell Butler and Maynard Dixon continued to paint and exhibit Zion's landscapes, assuring a place in the public imagination for this red rock world.

There were other efforts to increase visitation. A plan was hatched in the 1920s to create a road connecting Zion to Bryce and the Grand Canyon. The Zion–Mt. Carmel Tunnel blasted through a mile of solid rock, an engineering marvel at the time, creating a new east entrance to the park. A quirkier effort involved six University of Utah women. In June of 1919, the feminist movement had just earned women the right to vote. It was thought that six women, as the first tourists in the newly renamed Zion National Park, could reintroduce the public to its "gigantic grandeur." Their adventures were captured and published in national newspapers to promote the park. Despite their efforts, it took until 1975 for the park to reach one million annual visitors. With 4.3 million individuals visiting the park annually as of 2016, today's visitors may be nostalgic for those early days.

On our way to the next park, we stopped by Las Vegas, a common itinerary for many Zion visitors. Going from the serene quiet of Zion's dark night skies to an electric jungle, a land of neon lights and constant excess, was a jarring experience, but made us appreciate the national parks even more. In Las Vegas, there are sublime and wondrous experiences—lavish buffets, carnal pleasures—but they're available only at a high price. In the national parks, one can experience the Temple of Sinawava, the peaks of the Rockies, the history of this nation, maintained, preserved, and accessible to every American.

Here, are the stories from Zion—where the earth opens itself up and says, "Here's my story."

The Language of Zion

GREER K. CHESHER

Not long ago I sat in a small-town diner not far from here eating a small-town breakfast of fried eggs and hash browns when the European couple in the next booth waved the waitress over. A writer's job is to pay attention, and so I did, my ears growing like Pinocchio's nose. I unstuck my legs from the vinyl seat and scooted forward for a better view as the young, blonde daughter of the cook and owner bobbed to the couple's table.

"Do you have any stronger coffee?" the man implored through a thick accent, tilting his still-full cup toward her, its contents a translucent brown.

"Ahhh," she replied, "let me ask my mom."

Away she trotted to the kitchen, and I couldn't wait to see with what she would return. I was debating whether she had ever heard of espresso, something these folks probably injected, when she returned and smiling widely, said, "Here! Use as much as you like!" She triumphantly set a scoop of instant coffee crystals, tastefully presented in a small white bowl, on their table and whirled away. The couple leaned forward, stared at each other, then the bowl, and tentatively poked it with a spoon.

This is the Utah, and the Zion, I love.

Zion is its own country with its own language. This used to be truer than it is now, "There was a time when everyone spoke with a drawl, a southern twang almost, a western accent only heard now on the remotest ranches or from the oldest speakers. There are still young people, men mostly, who lean on their faded pickups in skinny-legged jeans, long-sleeved shirts buttoned at wrist and neck, and crisp cowboy hats who drawl into the long day about *bobwyr fentces, pert near everbody*, and *upta*, as in "I'm going *upta* Cedar City." But the influx of "accentless," English-speaking newcomers is changing all that.

Years ago I recall looking up a mystery plant *everbody* called *Sarvis berry*. It turned out to be the familiar serviceberry. I had to learn to pronounce Cedar City, not with the accent on the word city, but as *CEE-dercity*. The nearby town of Hurricane is not pronounced like a tropical storm, but as a word with its own force: *HURR-i-cun*. I had to learn to call junipers cedars and to say such things as "Oh for cute!" and "Oh my heck!" in polite company.

Language reveals much. And with it goes much more. A nuance of meaning, particularities of place, a way of inhabiting the world. Words evolve to fit a place, pronunciations become angled by cliff echoes, sharpened by rockfall, smoothed by water.

Who knows what delicate shades of meaning were lost with the Virgin Anasazi and Parowan Fremont tongues. Maybe they're preserved in the Tiwa, Tewa, Towa, Keres, Hopi, or Zuni languages still in use in Arizona and New Mexico's extant pueblos. The Virgin Anasazi and Parowan Fremont lived in and around Zion, on the Colorado Plateau's fringe, their world's western extent, looking out over western Utah and Nevada's Basin and Range province. I imagine they spoke words created by canyons, and those same canyons were brought to life by words. A people and language shaped by environment. I imagine Anasazi as a language of water—water dripping, water running, water falling, water talking. I hear it often.

Other languages existed here. We see them reflected in the canyon's names. The Paiute called it Mukuntuweap, the original meaning now obscure. There is Parunuweap Canyon ("a canyon with a swift stream"), the Pa'rus Trail (*PA-roos*, "white foaming water"; Parussi, "whirling water," the Virgin River), Mount Kinesava, and the Temple of Sinawava (in the Paiute creation story, heroes Wolf and Coyote are called Senangwav, a name that also translates as "God" or "Spirit").

Pioneer names resonate in places such as Behunin and Heaps Canyons, Crawford Wash, and Johnson Mountain. In 1916 Frederick Vining Fisher, a Methodist missionary and national park advocate, named the Great White Throne (God's Throne) and, with his local guide Claud Hirschi, the Three Patriarchs.

The Mormon faith echoes in Mount Moroni and Kolob Canyons. Zion, a word interpreted around these parts as "sanctuary," is borrowed from Hebrew.

Names reveal a history and a worldview. There are the practical: Horse Pasture Plateau and Corral Hollow; the directional: North and South Guardian Angel, East and West Temple; the descriptive: Pine Valley, Grapevine Spring, Wildcat Canyon, Coalpits Wash. In such beautiful places people often revert to the language of awe and grandeur: Mount Majesty, Castle Dome, Inclined Temple, Phantom Valley, Mountain of Mystery. And there are the unknown: LaVerkin Wash. LaVerkin? Nobody knows. What would we call the Great White Throne today?

Some Paiute call their homeland Tiwiinarivipi, the "Storied Land." In an ethnographic overview of Zion National Park, Paiute Angelita Bulletts says, "It is said that the plants, animals, and in fact, everything on this land, understands the Paiute language, and when one listens closely and intently enough, there is affirmation and a sense of understanding. The complexity of our culture lies in our ability to converse with the animals and the landscape in this land. It is believed that this ability will prove to be important for all mankind someday." The land, it is said, understands us. It is speaking to us all the time. The late Paiute Elder Clifford Jake said, "The land is waiting for our answer."

I want to tell you of this Zion. Of a land that speaks, that sings. I want you to hear the song of cottonwood whispering to the Virgin's waters. I want you to see the color of sunset on the cliffs in fall. I feel my language inadequate.

To tell you the story of Zion, to have you feel it, see it, I want a different way of talking, a new alphabet. I want a language full of exacting definition: a word for the precise pink of manzanita flowers in earliest spring, for the experimental green of cottonwoods leafing along the Virgin River, itself the dusty watercolor of spring runoff.

I want a word to convey the first touch of sun hot on winter-white flesh so you can feel it, smell it. Scratch-and-sniff words; hot words and cold; words jagged as a new-broken rockfall. Words that lie smooth as a waterworn pebble in your mind.

I want ink that, when held up to the light, glows like melon cut open in the sun, like light through a cactus petal. Ink that, when read, splashes off the page, river water around boulders. I want parchment the color of Indian ricegrass in June. I want a language of thunderstorm and baked sand.

I can only acquaint you with the conversation I've been having with this place for the last twenty years or so, and I can only use the language I have, inadequate though it may be. I carry a slight accent. Those from here can tell I'm not, but they can also tell that after all these years I am now *of* here.

Zion converses with mockingbird and desert tortoise, mountain lion and morning cloak. It twirls cliffrose plumes on its windy fingers while waiting to speak with you. Get yourself a cuppa coffee; let's talk. ✦

About This Story

The wonderful thing about language is that it molds from region to region to fit the needs of the people who speak it. Over a "cuppa coffee," Greer K. Chesher weaves her local dialect with a lost language and the geography that has inspired her so much of her spirituality. Living language fits a place that was once called Mukuntuweap, translated as "straight river," "sacred cliffs," or "straight arrow," only to be later named Zion by Mormon pioneer Isaac Behunin.

A former Zion park ranger, Greer is a Rockville, Utah, resident. Zion is a landscape of extremes and talking with Greer also made clear that it elicits intense emotion. While Greer may not be from here, she asserts that she is of this place. Her words oozed with the emotional investment that those who have spent time in Zion feel for the red rock. Again and again, our interviews turned emotional as we discussed what made this place special. Watching the emotion pour out of Greer as she sat across from us, it made sense why so much of the language of Zion is spiritual.

Why the North Star Stands Still

WILLIAM R. PALMER

Tu-omp-pi-av, the sky, is wonderful. It is like tu-weap, the earth. There are high mountains there with their tops pointing to us. There are rivers. There are trees. There are brush and grass and flowers. There is warm weather and there is cold weather. There are day and night. Tu-omp-pi-av is an inverted world above us.

Tu-omp-pi-av is full of living things. To the Indians they are poot-see, but we call them stars. They are restless like the Indians. They have traveled around and traveled around until they have made trails all over the sky. If we watch all through the night we will see which way they go.

Some of the stars are birds. They go away for a long time and then they come back. They have been wintering in some warmer land. Some are animals. They are hunting better grass. Quan-ants, the eagle, is there. Cooch, the buffalo, is there. Tu-ee, the deer, and cab-i, the horse, are there. All the good animals are there. Tu-omp-pi-av, the sky, is their happy hunting ground, and all of them are traveling, traveling, traveling, following the feed and the good weather.

But one great one is there who does not travel. He is Qui-am-i Wintook, the North Star. He cannot travel. There is no place that he can go. Once he was na-gah, the mountain sheep, on tu-weap, the earth. He was son of Shinob and beloved by him. He was daring. He was brave. He was surefooted. He was courageous. Shinob was proud of him and loved him so much that he put great earrings on the sides of his head to make him look dignified and commanding.

Always na-gah was climbing, climbing, climbing. He hunted out the roughest and the highest mountains, and there he lived and was happy. Once in the very long ago na-gah found a very high peak. Its sides were steep and smooth and its top was a high sharp peak reaching up into the clouds. Na-gah looked up and said, "I wonder what is up there. I will climb to the very highest point."

He set out to find a way up. Around the mountain and around the mountain he went seeking for a trail, but there was no trail. There was nothing but sheer cliffs all the way around. This was the very first mountain na-gah had ever seen which he could not climb.

He thought about it. He thought much about it. He worried about it. He would feel disgraced if Shinob knew there was a mountain that na-gah could not climb. The more he thought, the more he determined that he would find a way up to the top. Shinob would be proud to see him standing on the very top of such a mountain.

Around the mountain and around the mountain he went again and again. He went many times and always he was stopping to peer up the steep cliff to see if there was not a crevice or a narrow shelf on which he could find footing. At every such place he found, he went up as far as he could but always he came to a place beyond which he could not go and he had to turn around and come back. At last he found a big crack in the rock that went down and not up. Down into it he went. Soon he found a hole that turned up and his heart was glad. Up and up he climbed. Soon it grew so dark he could not see and the cave was full of loose rocks that slipped under his feet and rolled down. A great and fearsome noise as if the mountain were coming to pieces came up through the shaft as the rolling rocks dashed themselves to pieces at the bottom. In the darkness he slipped often and skinned and bruised his knees, and his courage began to fail. He was afraid. He had never seen any place so dark before.

Na-gah grew tired and said, "I will go back and look again for a better place to climb. I am not afraid out on the open cliffs but this dark hole fills me with fear. I am scared. I want to get out." But when na-gah turned to go down he found that the rolling rocks had closed the cave below him. He could not get down. There was only one thing now that he could do. He must go on climbing until he came out somewhere.

After a long time he looked up and saw a little light and he knew that he was coming out. He said, "Now I am happy. I am glad that I came through this dark hole." When at last na-gah came out into the open it almost took his breath. He was on the very top of a very high peak. There was scarcely room for him to turn around, and to look down from this great height made him dizzy. There were great cliffs below him all around and only a very small place for him to move around. Nowhere could he get down on the outside and the cave was closed on the inside. "Here," he said, "I must die, but I have climbed my mountain."

It was a bad situation he was in but there was a little grass for him to eat and there was water in the holes in the rocks. He ate and drank and then he felt better. He was higher than all the mountains he could see and he could look down on tu-weap, the earth.

About this time Shinob was out walking over tu-omp-pi-av, the sky. He looked all over for na-gah but could not find him. He called loudly for his son and na-gah answered from the top of the high cliffs. When Shinob saw him there, he felt sorrowful for he knew na-gah could never come down. Shinob said to himself, "My brave son can never come down. Always he must stand on top of the high mountain. He can travel and climb no more. Always he must stand on that little spot for there is no place he can go. I will not let my brave son die. I will turn him into poot-see, a star, and he can stand there and shine where everyone can see him. He shall be a guide mark for all the living things upon the earth or in the sky."

It was even so. Na-gah became a star that every living thing can see and the only star that will always be found in the same place. Directions are set by him and the traveler, looking at him, can always find his way. Always he stands still. He does not move around as the other stars do and because he is in the true north, the Indians call him "Qui-am-i Wintook Poot-see," the North Star.

There are other mountain sheep in tu-omp-pi-av, the sky.

We call them big dipper and little dipper. They too have found the great mountain and have been challenged by it. They have seen na-gah standing on the top and they want to go up to him. Shinob turned them also into stars and you may see them in the sky at the foot of the big mountain. Always they are traveling. They go round and round the mountain seeking the trail that leads upward to na-gah, who stands on the top. ✦

About This Story

The night sky has long been a source of speculation, and stories. For our ancestors, a lack of electricity offered brilliant views of the night sky, and time to ponder this strange, twinkling canopy. Today, Utah's national parks and monuments protect 60 percent of its land, making it one of the last great places in the world to view the night sky as our ancestors might have.

Why the North Star Stands Still is one of the most famous stories of the local Paiute tribes. It tells us of a daring and brave mountain sheep that ascends to become the North Star. We must note that this version is told in the collection of William R. Palmer, a European scholar who was taken into the tribe after securing better homes for them. In our interview with Paiute elder and park ranger Benn Pikyavit, he warned us that many versions of Paiute stories have been "Mormonized," or recorded and altered through the lens of Mormon values. But Benn pointed to Palmer's book as a fairly accurate collection of Paiute stories. He did also warn that if you tell these stories aloud in the summer, you run the risk of being visited by a rattlesnake . . . so read at your own risk!

The Coyote Clan

TERRY TEMPEST WILLIAMS

When traveling to southern Utah for the first time, it is fair to ask, if the redrocks were cut would they bleed. And when traveling to Utah's desert for the second or third time, it is fair to assume that they do, that the blood of the rocks gives life to the country. And then after having made enough pilgrimages to the slickrock to warrant sufficient separation for society's oughts and shoulds, look again for the novice you once were, who asked if sandstone bleeds.

Pull out your pocketknife, open the blade, and run it across your burnished arm. If you draw blood, you are human. If you draw wet sand that dries quickly, then you will know you have become part of the desert. Not until then can you claim ownership.

This is Coyote's country—a landscape of the imagination, where nothing is as it appears. The buttes, mesas, and redrock spires beckon you to see them as something other: a cathedral, a tabletop, bear's ears, or nuns. Windows and arches ask you to recall what is no longer there, to taste the wind for the sandstone it carries. These astonishing formations invite a new mythology for desert goers, one that acknowledges the power of story and ritual yet lies within the integrity of our own cultures. The stories rooted in experience become beads to trade. It is the story, always the story, that precedes and follows the journey.

Just when you believe in your own sense of place, plan on getting lost. It's not your fault—blame it on Coyote. The terror of the country you thought you knew bears gifts of humility. The landscape that makes you vulnerable also makes you strong. This is the bedrock of southern Utah's beauty: its chameleon nature according to light and weather and season encourages us to make peace with our own contradictory nature. The trickster quality of the canyons is Coyote's cachet.

When the Navajo speak of Coyote, they do so hesitantly, looking over their shoulders, checking the time of the year so they won't be heard. They know his stories are told only after the first frost and never after the last thaw. Their culture has been informed by Coyote. He is profane and sacred, a bumbler and a hero. He straddles the canyon walls with wild oats in his belly. And they know him by name—*Ma'ii*, the one never to be taken for granted. They understand his fickle nature, how he seduces fools into believing their own myths, that they matter to the life of the desert.

Coyote knows we do not matter. He knows rocks care nothing for those who wander through them; yet he also knows that those same individuals who care for the rocks will find openings—large openings—that become passageways into the unseen world, where music is heard through doves' wings and wisdom is gleaned from the tails of lizards. Coyote is always nearby but remains hidden. He is an ally because he cares enough to stay wary. He teaches us how to survive.

It is Coyote who wanders naked in the desert and leaves his skin on the highway, allowing us to believe he is dead. He knows sunburned flesh is better than a tanned hide, that days spent in the desert are days soaking up strength. He can retrieve his coat and fluff up his fur after a wild day in the wilderness and meet any man, woman, or child on the streets of Moab and seduce them for dinner. Coyote knows it is the proportion of days spent in wildness that counts in urbane savvy.

Coyote's howl about the canyon says the desert may not depend on his life, but his life depends on the desert.

We would do well to listen.

The canyons of southern Utah are giving birth to a Coyote Clan—hundreds, maybe even thousands, of individuals who are quietly subversive on behalf of the land. And they are infiltrating our neighborhoods in the most respectable ways, with their long, bushy tails tucked discreetly inside their pants or beneath their skirts.

Members of the Clan are not easily identified, but there are clues. You can see it in their eyes. They are joyful and they are fierce. They can cry louder and laugh harder than anyone on the planet. And they have enormous range.

The Coyote Clan is a raucous bunch: they have drunk from desert potholes and belched forth toads. They tell stories with such virtuosity that you'll swear you have been in the presence of preachers.

The Coyote Clan is also serene. They can float on their backs down the length of any river or lose entire afternoons in the contemplation of stone.

Members of the Clan court risk and will dance on slickrock as flash floods erode the ground beneath their feet. It doesn't matter. They understand the earth re-creates itself day after day.

The images and stories that follow [in *Red: Passion and Patience in the Desert*] come from Coyote's Canyon. They are dedicated to the Clan, to give them strength when they are away from the slickrock, to "jar their memories that beauty is not found in the excessive but in what is lean and spare and subtle." ✦

About This Story

Having only a tent to shelter us from a 110-degree heat wave that lasted well into the night may have spoiled our introduction to the desert. All we saw was endless rock, blazing sun, and a dryness that crept its way deep under our skin with no relief in sight.

It was Terry Tempest Williams's writing that opened our eyes to the beauty of the desert, something we desperately needed if we were going to last here. *The Coyote Clan* is an incredible rumination on the red rock country, and a celebration of those individuals who somehow find abundance and beauty in this seemingly desolate place. Zion is a place with extreme heat and extreme floods, but it is also a place that makes you strong.

Williams captures in her writing so much of what we were experiencing, but had failed to appreciate before seeing it through her perspective. Although we struggled at first, we rose to the challenge, and found much to love in the desert. And when we had learned enough, we checked into a motel for a few nights.

The Great White Throne—
Has It Ever Been Climbed?

ANGUS M. WOODBURY

"Did you hear about the man climbing the Great White Throne?" the Superintendent asked me.

"No! When did that happen?" I rejoined.

"They say a fellow went up to try it yesterday and didn't come back."

"Of course he didn't get up?"

"I don't know. They report seeing a fire on the Throne last night."

"Lightning." I answered, thinking of the recent thunderstorms.

"Well, let's go up to the campground and investigate."

As we went, my mind reverted to an attempt I had once made to climb that majestic monolith—the Great White Throne. I reviewed the details of that trip—how I had, with others, gone entirely around that gigantic rock and studied with an experienced eye every possible nook and cranny on all four faces. It was clearly impossible on the west and north faces where those vertical cliffs towered 2,500 feet from the canyon floor. Nor was it possible on the east side where another vertical wall 1,200 feet high overlooked the beautiful Hidden Canyon. On the south side, in the rear of the Throne—there was a possibility. The wall there was only a thousand feet high and it was not a vertical wall—merely a steep slope. But surely no one would be fool-hardy enough to climb such a slope! A loosened foothold might be a prelude to a free slide to the bottom.

Arriving at the campground, we soon found people who had seen the fires the night before. Standing at the foot of that majestic wall rising a sheer 2,500 feet above us, they pointed out as nearly as possible the location of the fires.

"We saw fires in two places," one man said. "First, it was on top at the left; later, it seemed to be over by the big arch, and one time, it looked like a fire falling through the arch. We thought it was a fire ball like you see in Yosemite and didn't pay much attention to it."

Knowing that the arch was several hundred feet below the top and that above it was a narrow shelf that would effectively stop any embers that fell from the top, I discounted the testimony and thought that, it being dark, they had not accurately located the fires.

We located the climber's partner and learned the story. His name was Evans and he was a great mountain climber. He was absolutely fearless and took no thought whatever of danger. Mountain slopes and precipices had an irresistible appeal, drawing him like a magnet. An unclimbed mountain was, to him, like bait to a hungry bear.

As soon as he heard that the Great White Throne had not been scaled, he could not rest until he made the attempt. The two had spent several days in the Park and Evans had spent much of the time studying the Throne from many angles. Two days before, he had reconnoitered the north face, but came back before noon. The following day, he had been up on the East Rim trail, spending much of his time studying the Throne. Then he had started out with the avowed purpose of scaling the height. He carried with him a short rope and a small canteen of water, but no food, saying that he would probably be late that night and might not be back until the next day. If he reached the top, as the fires indicated, he ought to be returning here by noon.

Excitement reigned. Rangers had gone out hunting his tracks, expecting to meet him or hear from him any minute. If he did not return by noon, then it would be time for action.

The rangers returned by noon and reported no word from him. They had, however, found his tracks and knew which route he had taken. His silence was ominous! If he were alive and unharmed, he could, in all probability, have heard us shouting, so the probability was that something had happened. We must start an immediate search for him.

A consultation followed. The consensus of opinion placed him in the canyon at the south rear of the Throne where the lone possibility of climbing it lay. But that canyon was 1,500 feet above us at the top of precipitous walls. How to get to it was the question.

Ruesch was for taking horses around the East Rim trail and coming back over the plateau from the rear. A good suggestion if we had more time. I was for taking his tracks above the Grotto and around to the foot of the Throne, the shortest and quickest way, but there was one bad place we dared not climb without a ladder.

"We can soon make a ladder," said Ruesch. And so it was agreed.

When the ladder was ready, willing hands carried it up the angular slope through the heavy brush to the foot of the bad ledge. It was on a narrow shelf on which there was just room enough to stand. Below was a steep slope leading down to the top of a vertical cliff 300 feet high. Carefully, very carefully, the ladder was raised into position. The foot was not solid. We picked a hold for it to rest in. Dalton stood behind and helped hold it in place. Russell held the foot to keep it from slipping.

Cautiously, I started up the ladder. Near the top I hesitated. Dalton was shaking in his shoes.

"For God's sake, man, do be careful," from Russell.

And: "I wouldn't go up that damn thing for ten thousand dollars," from Ruesch.

The 16 feet of ladder was not long enough and I knew it. I could not climb over a hump just above its top. I stood there pondering. Far below, on the road near the campground a group of people were anxiously watching, among them our congressman. At the foot of the ladder were a group of veteran mountaineers deprecating the attempt. Somewhere on the mountain-side above a young man was probably writhing in agony if no worse fate had befallen him. Something must be done!

A dramatic moment! I could not go forward and I could not admit defeat! If there were only a rope fastened from above, anyone could climb it. We knew by his tracks that Evans had gone this way without any help, but no one in the group was willing to take the unwarranted risks that he had taken. I looked carefully for possibilities. Over on the left, was a crevice—a crack in the rock full of possibilities—if one could only get to it. If the ladder were laid down and used as a bridge, I could make it.

I slowly descended. We lowered the ladder across to the foot of the crevice. Carefully, cautiously, I walked across whereas Evans had blithely stepped around a sloping rock upon which a slipping foot would have meant sudden death. I climbed up through the crack, fastened the rope and dropped one end down over the ladder which had in the meantime been replaced. Gifford came up with the aid of the rope and we were then ready for the hunt.

Following Evans' tracks, we hurried on into the canyon above the Grotto. His tracks continued on up the bottom apparently leading into a blind canyon. We decided not to follow them but to go directly over to the foot of the Throne, the shortest way possible and pick up his tracks over there. We climbed over the hogsback on the left and dropped down into the next deep gorge. The exit was not so easy. Scaling some precarious ledges, crannies, and crevices, we reached the top of the next ridge and soon made our way over to the foot of the Throne.

We skirted the foot where Evans should have gone up. No signs and no tracks could we find. We tested the slope to see if it were possible to climb it. Walking up some distance, we found it easy to ascend but dangerous coming back down. Skirting the foot in the opposite direction still looking for tracks, we soon came out on the ledge above the campground and signalled "No luck."

We were puzzled. A man could not disappear without leaving tracks. If he did not get to the Throne, where could he be? Looking back into the canyon where we had left Evans' tracks, we could see the blind canyon into which he had gone. To us, it seemed that a human could not possibly climb out of it. We had taken the only other alternative route and were positive that he had not come out that way. The inference was that since his tracks led into a blind canyon, he must still be there. Our hope then lay in following his tracks till we found him.

It was nearly dark when we had returned to the point where we had left his tracks, and knowing that we could do nothing in the ledges in the darkness, we went down for the night. We reached the foot of the ladder in safety, but the darkness had become so intense that we could not find our way down for fear of the ledges below us. Russell came up with a flashlight and led us down. The crowd at the foot were anxiously waiting for word that we had not to give.

Tired and weary, I tossed on my couch all night long, thinking of the possibilities of a lad alone in the mountains and trying to solve the riddle of his strange disappearance. Had we missed his tracks? Had he strayed and got lost? Had he fallen and injured himself? Was he still in that blind canyon? Or had he reached the Throne as the fires seemed to indicate? We would find an answer on the morrow.

By dawn, I was up getting ready for a new day's hunt. Ruesch, Russell, and Gifford took horses up the East Rim trail planning to come back over the plateau above looking for his tracks. Shieffer and I planned to follow his tracks up through that blind canyon. We climbed the ladder in safety and took his tracks up the canyon. Near the head, we encountered a snowdrift (June 29) protected by the mighty cliffs above. Just beyond, the canyon narrowed to a vertical slit—a chimney—300 feet high and just wide enough to admit a human body.

Above the slit and underneath the overhanging cliff, a buzzard was soaring around. Knowing the carrion-eating habits of the bird, horrid pictures of ugly possibilities flashed through our minds. It was imperative that we go on, up through that slit where Evans' tracks led, much as we hated to do so.

With back against one wall and feet braced against the other, we wriggled our way up through that chimney-like slit in the cliffs. On top, the climbing was worse than ever. Expecting to find the end of our search at any minute, we continued along his tracks upward, ever upward. The buzzard was gone and his story was a lie—we knew when we reached the open slope at the head of the canyon. But here, the danger of slipping and rolling was so great that even Shieffer balked.

"Well Woodbury, there's no sense in one of us going over the edge and I'm not going any farther."

While debating what to do, we heard the horsemen yell from above indicating important information but we could not understand clearly what they said. Inferring that they had found his tracks on top of the plateau, we felt that there would be no further use for us to continue. We retreated down through the slit to the bottom of the canyon and climbed out on the ridge that I had crossed the day before.

Just across the next deep box canyon, a quarter mile distant, the horsemen were waiting for us to appear. We could easily hear them. Russell shouted: "We found his tracks where they came out of the canyon and followed them around the plateau to the edge of the canyon behind the Throne. There, they dropped off into the head of the canyon where it's awful steep and rough." It was the worst place he could have chosen to get into the canyon.

"He must be over in that canyon where we were hunting for him yesterday. He can't be any other place," I said. "You had better go in and see."

"Alright," returned Russell. "You wait there until we come back."

And right glad we were to do so. A chance to rest was welcome news after our heavy exertions of the morning.

A half-hour later, about 3 o'clock, he came back and shouted, "We've found him and he's alive. Come over as quick as you can."

Before leaving, we went down to the ledge overlooking the Grotto and gave the signal that he had been found—three yells in succession. The superintendent below getting the message telegraphed to the nation that he had been found.

It took us just an hour to cross that deep gorge a quarter-mile across. In the meantime, Ruesch, Russell, and Gifford had made a stretcher and carried him out of the brush where they had found him at the foot of the Throne about 50 yards beyond where we searched for him the day before.

And when we came to him, what a sight! Clothes nearly gone; lacerated, bruised, and sandpapered; his face a mass of sores; one eye swelled shut; but apparently no bones broken. Undoubtedly delirious, he talked to us but there was no coherence to his speech. He could tell us nothing about his trip.

With four men hold of the stretchers—the fifth man taking turns—we carried him out of that thousand-foot canyon.

We did the best we could, but whenever a limb or a bush scrubbed a sore spot, he swore as only a true sailor can.

Reaching the top at 5 p.m., we put him on one of the horses and with a man on behind to hold him in place, we rode around the plateau and down the East Rim trail. Arriving at the foot of the trail at 10 p.m., many willing hands were ready to transfer him to a waiting ambulance which took him to the Lodge, where three doctors were ready to care for him.

At the end of two weeks, they took him home to Pasadena, where he spent many weeks convalescing in the hospital. While in Zion, he regained but a few lucid moments during the entire two weeks stay.

Did he reach the top? It is an open question. During his lucid moments in Zion, it was possible to pry out a few details of his trip, and after his return home, further details filtered back to us. It has thus been possible to piece together the outlines of his story.

He thinks he reached the top about dark, built a fire, and the wind blew embers down onto the shelf above the arch, where a new fire started. He climbed down to put it out and in doing so knocked embers down through the arch. Finding shelter on top in a small cave, he stayed there all night. On the rock he carved his name and a warning to other fools who made the trip. At daylight, he started down. At one point along the way, he attempted to slide from one bush to the next, but missed it and remembered nothing more. His watch stopped about 5 o'clock and he was found the next day at 3 p.m.—34 hours later. One of the doctors stated that it was a good thing—the delay in finding him—as the rest gave him a better chance for recovery from brain concussion.

"Did he get to the top?" exclaimed a skeptic. "I'm not sold on the idea. When someone else goes up there and finds his name carved on the rock, then I'll believe it. Until then no one can make me believe that he did not fall going up!" ✦

About This Story

A search for a missing climber, the race against time—the elements of this story, set against Zion's tallest peak, the Great White Throne, felt like a classic campfire tale. Walter Ruesch, the first superintendent of Zion, who was responsible for the Walter's Wiggles trail at Angels Landing, also makes an appearance in this story.

Everything in the desert is extreme. The heat is one obvious factor, but there are also flash floods to keep the search and rescue team busy. During our Zion trip, we watched search and rescue get ready to retrieve someone from The Narrows, a famous hike that is a must-see under the right weather conditions.

As demonstrated in this story, the lure of the unconquerable is a constant draw of the natural world. Woodbury recalls the search for a man who pushed himself to reach the summit of the Great White Throne, and the team of men who helped him return home.

The Ghosts of Zion

J. L. CRAWFORD

My childhood haunts keep beckoning to me.
Those playgrounds of my youth I long to see;
   But the routine of my day bids fancy wait
Until the canyon's call shall find me free.

Today I heard the call and came at last.
The spell of sweet nostalgia held me fast,
   And, giving in to pleasant reverie,
I mingled with the ghosts of Zion past.

In a grotto where I'd often been before,
I sat and dreamed, and let my spirit soar
   To bygone days and other scenes I knew,
As through a gossamer veil I shared the canyon's lore.

There was Nephi Johnson and his Paiute guide,
Who stayed at Oak Creek and refused to ride
   Into the place where the feared Wainopits dwells,
And would wait there only until eventide.

There appeared the image of one I didn't know,
Who stood awhile to watch the passing show.
   Then I recognized the ghost of Joseph Black,
When he winked at me and said, "I told you so."

"And I told my friends that someday they'd be sorry,
When the world would come and listen to my story.
    They laughed at me and said that I was daft,
And called my beautiful canyon 'Joseph's Glory'."

Near a place where Mount Majestic stands,
I saw Behunin, Heap and Rolf plow the river sands,
    And Isaac name his haven "Little Zion"
With temples built by God and not by hands.

I wondered why those stalwarts moved away,
While many other builders came to stay.
    But, here or there, they left their marks in passing,
And I felt their spirits' presence here today.

In my mind's eye there was one familiar scene
Of sweating men—determined, bronzed and lean—
    Who built houses, roads, diversion dams and ditches,
As through their toil they made the valley green.

Then came the U. S. Geological Survey,
Whose photographers, artists and writers would convey
    To all mankind the beauty of this place.
Then it was plain the world was here to stay.

Next, men of foresight came and made a park
Of nature's gem; where soon I would embark
    Upon my life's career, and get my start
Where many men in green have left their mark.

I saw many Superintendents come and go,
And greeted everyone I chanced to know;
    Also my many pals at Zion Lodge—
Those friendships that I made I won't outgrow.

I shook hands with a President and movie star.
Crown Prince of Sweden came in chauffeured car.
    All this I hope to someday see again,
As I leave the doorway to my past ajar.

I thought to take my leave as day was done;
To come again and see if I had won
    A favored place; but paused again to see
A golden glow cast by a setting sun.

I turned and said, "Greetings, old Flanigan Peak."
A voice came back, "Take care to whom you speak,
    Brash upstart, you will not find here
The gift of immortality you seek."

"In tales you tell and pictures that you paint,
Your forebears oft appear without a taint;
    But while you venerate ancestral lore,
Antiquity alone does not make one a saint."

"Those ghosts of yesterday with whom you talk
Are merely squatters in this land, and mock
    The sanctity of these enduring shrines;
For flesh is not as durable as rock."

"Frail man, look quickly at my alpenglow;
For you shall pass, much as the winter snow.
    Long after you have gone I'll keep my watch.
I saw the Anasazi come and go."

"Great Watchman, I look up to you." I said,
But let me also love my kindred dead,
    And all whose sweat and toil built thoroughfares
On which the feet of all the world now tread.

"I'll worship at these temples, not built by man,
And sing about their splendor while I can.
　　But I would give the pioneer his due."
And the mountain smiled approval of my plan.

Then as I left I thought about my day;
And all my friends of now and yesterday.
　　I know their deeds are graven in the stone;
Instead of lightly scribbled in the clay.

As long as I can feel and hear and see
I'll come here oft, just save a nook for me.
　　And when these senses dim, I'll take my place
Among the ghosts of Zion yet to be. ✦

About This Story

Families who are displaced by the creation of a national park can sometimes have a bittersweet relationship with the park. But for J. L. Crawford, a Mormon settler whose family sold their farm to the National Park Service, working as a park ranger was also the best way to celebrate his childhood, he spent in what is now the back patio of the Zion Human History Museum.

Crawford channels that unique point of view into this poem, written for the seventy-fifth anniversary of Zion National Park. Crawford recalls the spirituality that his Mormon ancestors felt in this canyon. He reflects on the ancient wisdom of the landscape, the Mormon discovery of this canyon, and the history of his ancestors settling in this place. When challenged by the landscape itself, Crawford humbly asks the spirits if he might haunt this land he loves.

YOSEMITE NATIONAL PARK

A Cathedral of Granite

THE FIRST FEDERALLY protected land in the world, this iconic and awe-inspiring park is full of many firsts—from developing the concept of what it means to manage and protect land, to inspiring some of the modern world's best climbing gear, as the landscape lends itself to being an adventurer's playground.

illustration by
JOSIE PORTILLO

wo weeks before we arrived in Yosemite, the Obamas visited for Father's Day weekend. President Barack Obama stood in front of the tallest waterfall in North America to say: "There's something sacred about this place, and I suppose that's why the walls of this valley were referred to as cathedral walls, because here at Yosemite we connect not just with our own spirit, but with something greater. It's almost like the spirit of America itself is right here."

He's not the first president to proclaim the beauty of this place. A hundred years earlier, Theodore Roosevelt spent three nights camping in Yosemite with naturalist John Muir. Fifty years prior to that, Abraham Lincoln considered the petition of a group of Californians, arguing for the preservation of Yosemite's larger-than-life sequoia trees and granite. Responding to the petitions, paintings, and photographs, Lincoln, during one of the bloodiest periods of the Civil War, put pen to paper and signed the Yosemite Grant in 1864. Since then, the nation has been learning what it means to both protect a place's wildness and make it accessible to visitors. Yosemite is where we, as a nation, figured out what a national park would be. That awkward, beautiful, sometimes painful process has produced countless stories.

After returning from our trip, everyone wanted to know what our favorite park was. Choosing just one felt easy and impossible at the same time. Acadia has our hearts, but Yosemite has our imagination. Swept up in the romance of its past, we quickly felt part of Yosemite's community. Living here is not just a different pace of life, but a different set of values. One's riches aren't measured in salary, but by accumulated adventures and experiences. It's that "dirt on your feet" attitude that binds the community together in towns like El Portal, Foresta, Mariposa, Tuolumne, and Mono Lake. Every other Thursday, Sal's Taco Night in El Portal draws a raucous local crowd. The Mobil Gas Station, just past Tuolumne Meadows, has bands every Thursday night; we were invited on a midnight trip to nearby hot springs afterward.

Our research required us to stay in the park campgrounds, but we also spent time in Mariposa, the gateway town to Yosemite. On a friend's Mariposa property, we set up home base in a tent cabin: the kind you see on iconic Curry Village postcards. The cabin provided a dependable roof over our heads, a real mattress with down blankets, string lights overhead, and our friend's dog, Banjo, proudly

named by Ilyssa years before, as our security detail. After months of pitching a
tent, it was a luxury to not have to find the perfect campsite with proximity to a
bathroom—a trip Ilyssa now needed to make every few hours to accommodate the
human growing inside of her. The property is over 360 acres, with opportunities
for brilliant stargazing or moonlit hikes. These sights had us longing for a time
machine to take us back to the romantic days of Yosemite that locals shared with
us—notably, the Yosemite Firefall. Every evening in Curry Village, David Curry,
dressed in a dapper white suit as the "stentor," would shout up to Glacier Point:
"Let the fire fall!" At this cue, a colleague stationed on the 3,200-foot peak of
Glacier Point would push the embers of a fire off the edge, creating a spectacular
waterfall of fire, an orange streak that streamed down to the valley below, while a
pianist played the "Indian Love Call" from nearby Ahwahnee Hotel. Though the
Yosemite Firefall no longer operates, these events are remembered by visitors,
one of the myths of a magical park that once was.

Standing on the floor of Yosemite Valley, it's hard to imagine anything bigger
than the granite cliffs above. On that first drive into the park, we were struck by
the beauty of the Valley, then left speechless by a glimpse of El Capitan. You can
find higher cliffs elsewhere in the world, but the spectacle of granite cliffs shooting
straight up from the floor of Yosemite Valley is unmatched. For many, Yosemite
is a playground for "adult childhoods"—a time when one is just old enough to
decide where to live, but young enough to not yet have careers, children, or
many cares. While some staff live in the modest accommodations provided by
Yosemite's hotels, others live out of vans, on a friend's property, in tents, or on
the side of the road. It's that enticing to be here.

The stable climate, sheer cliff faces, and accessibility brought rock climbers
from all over the world to Yosemite, revolutionizing the sport during the "Golden
Age" of Yosemite climbing from 1955 to 1970. That adventuring spirit still per-
meates this wilderness. In our brief stay in Yosemite, we saw slackliners setting
up on the edge of the Taft Point fissures, and spotted two "diving boards" from
which hang gliders (legally) and BASE jumpers (illegally) launch. These are in
addition to the hikers, backpackers, and peak baggers who tramp through the
95 percent of the park which is wilderness. Yosemite's granite is so alluring that
even those who haven't yearned to climb mountains find themselves anxiously

waiting to see if their number is selected in the Half Dome lottery—like Dave did, along with Ilyssa's brother, Sean, and his partner, Megan.

In the early 2000s, Half Dome saw one thousand hikers a day, making a dangerous trail even more so through overcrowding. After intensive studies, the Park introduced a permit system, limiting access to 350 hikers a day. Afraid of heights, and exhausted from the seven-hour hike to reach the final ascent, Dave wasn't thrilled about tackling Half Dome. But an opportunity to see Yosemite from the top could not be missed. Pulling himself up the cables, and clinging to the side of the cliff, Dave realized two things: that he needed to stay alive for his child, and that he wanted a daughter.

Just as it inspired Dave's first climbing experience, Yosemite has blazed trails throughout its history, with no precedent to follow, no maps or guides. The Yosemite Grant established the first protected natural land in the world. Likewise, much of the rock climbing equipment in use today was first developed on Yosemite's walls. Due to the growing popularity of the sport, particularly in Yosemite, an official search and rescue was formally organized to rescue stranded climbers. Beyond climbing, the Yosemite Natural History Association was the very first nonprofit partner to raise funds to support the park in 1923. Their first project was the Yosemite Museum, which was in turn the first to collect and interpret cultural artifacts, marking a shift in the conservation ideology of national parks. As bears learned that humans have food, park rangers pioneered a high-tech management program that alerts rangers whenever a bear enters a highly populated area. We were alerted by less sophisticated technology.

We had stopped to eat peanut butter and banana sandwiches at the top of Sentinel Dome, when we heard the snapping of twigs behind us. We turned around and spotted a black bear (which in Yosemite are actually brown), with a bright yellow tracking tag on its ear. Luckily for our party, the bear seemed to have no interest in us. Even so, one glimpse of this majestic animal impressed upon us why the black bear is so storied.

So many different people draw different lessons from this landscape, whether they search for them or not. Some ponder the place of humans in the universe. Some reflect on the act of preservation and how a group of people protected a place for us to enjoy, for all eternity. This landscape will teach, if you'll slow down to listen.

lombard gate

SHELTON JOHNSON

"**S**ergeant Yancy," said Second Lieutenant Rubottom, "get the stock ready, and inform the men that we're heading out."

"Beg your pardon, sir, but headin' where?" I asked.

He swiveled his head away toward the east. "Troop K has been ordered to Yosemite, Sergeant Yancy, and we're going to make the best of a bad assignment."

I thought a minute and then asked, "What's Yosemite?"

"*Yo-sem-i-te,*" began Rubottom wearily, stretching out the word till each syllable stood by itself, "is a thing called a national park, bout two hundred miles from here, up in the Sierra Nevada."

Every time Rubottom answered a question, he had a habit of making new ones. It wasn't easy talking to the man. I had no idea what a national park was, but the train that brought us to the Presidio from Florida had taken us through California's Sierra Nevada, a range of big mountains to the east that even now, in May, were all buried in snow.

Rubottom seemed in a hurry, as usual. Being around him made me anxious cause it felt like something was about to happen, even though nothing usually did. Now he looked like he wanted to be gone, but I had another question.

"Lieutenant Rubottom, sir. What's a national park?"

"Yancy," said Rubottom, "a national park is a problem for the United States Army created by the secretary of the Interior. At least that's how General MacArthur sees it, and I agree with the general, but unfortunately the secretary of war feels that Troops I, K, L, and M will provide a suitable solution. Now do you understand?"

"Yes sir!" I said. I didn't, but it seemed best to pretend I did, or I'd just hear more questions dressed up as answers.

"Good," Rubottom continued. "Now, in two hours I will have prepared detailed instructions regarding our departure from the Presidio, and I expect that you will carry out these instructions with your usual zeal. Do you understand?"

"Yes sir!" I said again. Responding with a "no sir!" when an officer's expecting a "yes sir!" usually just led to misery.

"That's fine, Sergeant," said Rubottom, sounding like a mule with colic. "Well, those are our orders, but we must hope that someone like MacArthur can conceive a way to countermand this ridiculous assignment, so we can get to the real work of the military." He walked away muttering what might have been curses. Rubottom had always been short-tempered, with a very low opinion of anything or anyone other than Rubottom.

I still didn't know what a national park was or what I would be doing with the rest of Troop K in Yosemite, but claiming ignorance was not a bad strategy when things went to hell and Rubottom was looking for someone to blame.

In less than two days we were on the move, equipped for extended duty in a place few of us had ever heard of. A farrier at the Presidio told me the army had been in Yosemite since 1891, protecting the park during the summer months. He said this national park wasn't like something you'd find in San Francisco. Apparently Yosemite was more than a grassy area with fountains and shade trees, so I thought it was strange they called it a park. Folks went all that distance just to take in the scenery, but I guess some took a little more than that, like timber or deer, and others had been grazing livestock there illegally. That's why the park needed protecting. I guess winter took over that duty once the soldiers left.

I still didn't know enough to look forward to the destination, but I looked forward to the change. Being away from a garrison with its endless drills and inspections would be a relief, even if Yosemite was, according to Rubottom, "a waste of military time."

I've forgotten most of that farewell day in San Francisco, but I do remember the slow ride out from the Presidio, up the winding road from the stables in columns of two, the hard clatter of hooves on harder ground, the creaking of caissons and wagons as the mules strained to pull them along, and the band playing "The Girl I Left Behind Me." What I can't forget, though, is a short conversation with some sentries when we finally got to the Lombard Gate of the Presidio. As we rode through, a couple of mules ahead of us got into an altercation, so we had to stop while the teamsters calmed them down. I heard the sentries talking.

"How come these niggers get to go to Yosemite?" one asked.

"Yeah," commented the other, "that's a plum duty and it's going to niggers instead of white soldiers. There are days I just don't understand the army."

It was right about then that my opinion of Yosemite began to improve.

"Hey, boys," I shouted to the soldiers, "I hear the fishin is pretty good up in the Sierra. If you're nice, maybe I'll bring you back some catfish or bass or maybe trout. I can't say which cause I just don't know what-all's up there in those mountains, but I figure we'll have plenty of time to find out!"

Some of the boys riding behind me started laughing, but not those sentries. I couldn't hear their comments once we started up again, cause the noise drowned out their voices, but I could see the meaning plainly written on their faces. It was a sight to make you smile.

It felt real nice to be starting the trip with the warm regard of my comrades. I was feeling pretty good bout myself till I turned in the saddle and looked straight into the glare of Second Lieutenant Rubottom, who was looking back at me with contempt. *Contempt* is a word the lieutenant likes using and demonstrating, particularly in regard to me. In this case the translation roughly meant, "Yancy, I'm going to make you wish you'd never been born!"

That's what's so wonderful bout military life. After a while, officers get to know you so well they don't even have to talk anymore, they can just hit you over the head with a look. Must be special training cadets get at West Point, to get their faces to communicate so clearly what ain't proper to say. The second lieutenant must've scored high on that drill.

San Francisco was cold, but the coldness coming off Rubottom was going to give me frostbite if it lasted much longer. Still, it was worth it just to see those sentries choke.

Maybe Yosemite wouldn't be so bad after all. ✦

horse heaven

SHELTON JOHNSON

Everyone's got a favorite place, a place that's who you are, and you can move through it, breathe the air, walk the ground, and be home in a way that you're not anyplace else. I found a place like that in Yosemite, or it found me.

It was a high meadow so close to the sky that the blue of heaven began to stain the plants below. You could see it in the high grass and flowers with the blue of the sky in their petals. Sky was so close there, maybe it was leaching its color, so after a rain the plant just pulls it from the air and gets drunk on it, waving back and forth in the breeze, giddy with indigo.

You'd be giddy too if you could walk there with snowy mountains rising round you, holding the trees in place. It was high and rocky and green and cold. Even in the sun it seemed cold and warm at the same time. Some places can hold opposite things, like putting something to your lips that's hot and cold and sweet and bitter, that's what that meadow was like. It was cold as if winter was walking out but warm as if spring was strolling in, and when they passed each other, they stopped and turned round, then spoke in the heart of it, comparing notes. It was a long conversation. You could hear their talk in the grass and in the trees and inside yourself.

Why was it so different from a thousand other meadows? I figure God's walked in all of them, but in this one he lingered. He slowed down from all his work, looked round, and said, "Now this is it!"

There's all kinds of quiet. There's the kind after a preacher prays to God in church, and the kind in Grandma Sara's room after she'd tell Death off. There's the kind round sunset when everything seems to take a deep breath and slowly let go. There's the early morning kind right before birds begin to sing. The quiet in this meadow had some of all those and more, even more variety than sound has. Out here you can school yourself on quiet, get to know all the varieties, like how Mr. Muir can tell you the name of every bird and every flower, talk about them as if they were people he knew.

If all those different kinds of quiet could be put in bottles, sealed shut, and set on a cellar shelf, that's what I'd do with this vintage in Yosemite. Then from time to time I'd open one up and drink down the quiet of that meadow, fill up with it, and no matter how angry or sad I was, I couldn't stay that way.

Yosemite taught me that silence is a sound, the best kinda sound cause it makes you listen not only to what's happening on the outside but what's really going on inside. Usually the inside was a place I didn't want to hear from too much, it'd be like feeling round the inside of a coffin to see if it would be comfortable. There would be plenty of time to get used to the feel of that. But in the silence of that meadow, I didn't mind hearing what was in my bones and my blood and my heart.

Anyway, I remember how riding into Horse Heaven would make me feel, how it would slow me down, calm me, soothe me like an ointment spread over a hurt I didn't even know I had.

I'd get off my mule, wrap the reins round his neck, and just let him go. There was always plenty to eat, so I was never afraid of him wandering off. That mule never looked happier than he was in Horse Heaven. I can still see flowers trailing from Satan's mouth, like he was puking a rainbow, and his head bobbing up and down, side to side, as he rambled round that meadow.

I didn't like it so much in the spring. Then the ground would be wet like it was remembering when it used to be a real lake, and the mosquitoes made the air hum like the strings of a banjo plucked by the Almighty himself. Then it was more like Horse Hell.

No, I mean late summer, when all the water had seeped back down into the ground, and you could lie back in the wildflowers after a long day in the saddle, and the pressure of your body would crush the purple under the red under the yellow of all those flowers, and squeeze the colors out into the air, and you could smell the flowers you couldn't see. They'd fill up your head and your lungs and someplace inside that was open and waiting.

As my eyes would close, I'd hear my mule pulling up plants, chewing noisily, the wind in the trees away over somewheres, and the droning of bees gathering pollen. I could see every blade of grass up close, a little black ant crawling up this one, a caterpillar ringed with yellow and black on that one, I could see it all up close and all far away. And me opening up to the blue, a big ring of blue bordered by pine branches, dark and green. I was right there in the center of that meadow, the center of the world.

You can see why I never took anyone else to Horse Heaven, or wrote about it in any ledger. Other soldiers and, worst of all, officers might've got curious, figured they needed to investigate. That would've ruined everything.

But even though I went there alone, I never felt alone. The grass was good company, and the flowers too. Birds were always flitting round. I noticed how a bird's song goes with what it looks like. Some birds don't stay on a note too long, as if they know it'll give way and collapse under the strain. Other birds say the same thing over and over again, like maybe it ain't getting listened to proper, so the bird's got to keep repeating what it's saying over and over till it does get heard.

It's not an easy thing to tell the truth, but birds make a song out of it, and sing it wherever they go.

The best time is the morning.

There are two sunrises in the Sierra Nevada. The second one is the one you see. It's when blackness fades in the east to a softness that ain't really a color, but then deepens to a color there ain't really a name for. Call it a distant relative of red, one that don't come round to visit very often but who's always welcome.

That cousin of red lightens to a yellow, and about then a wind often picks up, stirring the leaves and branches. You start seeing the outlines of trees that went away the night before as darkness took them. After a bit there's no doubt the sun is pulling itself up into heaven like an old man with a lamp climbing Jacob's ladder. That's the second dawn.

The first one is the one only birds see. Light has barely, barely leaked into the sky when they start up like a choir on Sunday. Bird eyes must be sharp to see it, or maybe they feel something so thrilling in that moment they can't help singing. Sometimes the whole forest echoed with what they were saying, and how long have they been saying those things?

I remember thinking maybe it was the birds who coaxed the sun out of bed and up that long stairway. The music would rise up and up, wave after wave, and the sun would follow, rising into a color that was just becoming blue, and I couldn't tell who was happier, the birds to see the sun or the sun to hear the music of those birds.

Maybe I was the happiest one, just to be there watching and listening. If you're a cavalryman and you find a heaven for horses, then you really have found paradise. I don't know, and maybe I don't want to know. Corporal Bingham taught me that thinking is good, but you can't forget to feel. When horses are tasting the wind, they're not thinking, and they never seem to worry about what they don't know.

In Yosemite, for the first time I was all right with not knowing. Usually I try to figure out something I ain't too clear on. I want to know how much it weighs, will it float, can you set it on fire, or what's it good for, but here I never looked for a reason or an answer. Some things you don't ask God. You don't say *why* to a lupine or a poppy or a shooting star, *thank you* will do just fine.

Some people call Yosemite a wilderness, but all that really means is it's a place where nothing ever stands alone but always got company, kind of like being in the military. No soldier is ever alone, cause he's got all the men in his troop. They're part of his squadron, which is part of a battalion, which is part of the Ninth Cavalry, and all those men are your family. People who will take a bullet meant for you, those people are your family. Someone who will die for you is your brother, and you're all bound to something bigger than you. You all belong to the regiment, you're all Ninth Cavalrymen, and that means something in the world.

The same thing's going on in this meadow. The grass is part of the ground, and the ground keeps the trees standing tall, and the trees hold the nests of birds, and the blue sky is beyond and between the branches of those lodgepole pines. Small things always add up to something bigger, and it never really ends. Too bad I can't see it all. Too bad I can't smell every flower. Too bad I can't hear all the music there is to hear in these woods. Too bad I'm running out of time.

That's what I always thought about in that meadow in the sky. I was running out of time. When I was there, I noticed flowers dancing in the breath of God one day, and those same flowers dull and shriveled the next. That made me think I needed to dance more, feel the wind on me, and the sun, before I went all dull and shriveled.

The place I called Horse Heaven got a real name on a map, but I'm not going to say it. You keep the whereabouts of your best fishing holes to yourself. Yeah, I went fishing in that meadow, but I was the bait at the end of the line. I was what was tossed into the high grass pushed into waves by a wind I can't feel no more. And something took the bait, took me, and pulled me up time and again into Horse Heaven.

All I got to do is think about it, and I'm there.

Everybody needs a place like that. Even Satan. Even an army mule. ✦

About These Stories

When Shelton Johnson first came to Yosemite, he was looking for his identity. A creative writing major from Detroit, part American Indian and part African American, Shelton sought a calling. In Yosemite, he stumbled across a photo of a Buffalo Soldier, and learned of an African American cavalry unit dispatched to protect Yosemite from poachers and timber thieves in 1899. And only a handful of people had ever heard of them.

This wasn't acceptable. Shelton had found his calling, and dedicated his career to increasing awareness of the Buffalo Soldiers. We attended his program at the Yosemite Theater, and got to see Johnson as Elizy Boman, reminiscing about his job protecting the park as one of the first African American park rangers. After appearing in the Ken Burns documentary on the national parks, Shelton has become one of the most famous park rangers in the country. And it's well deserved—without his advocacy, the Buffalo Soldiers would have remained forgotten.

Notes from my Tuolumne Journal

WILLIAM L. NEELY

I write of a certain rebellious spirit in Nature. The sentimental often speak of the calm and peace of the mountains and the never-changing tranquility of life up here, "away from our rapidly-changing civilization."

They are lulled.

If you are alert you will find that Nature is always redoing her hair and shifting the furniture around. She is never satisfied with the course of a stream through the meadows and is forever washing down the granites with floods and freshets, and ringing up a howling good thunderstorm when things get too dull.

I admire the coyote. Unlike introspective man, he never analyzes his actions or worries about his conflicts with the world, nor nurses regrets for yesterday's mistakes. He is forever in the present. One finds this healthy attitude all through nature. When the hawk is near, the birds set up an agitated racket. He swoops down and carries off a sparrow. When he is gone there is some fluttering about, but soon from some tree a song is heard again and business resumes.

The coyote faces the day . . . he never yearns for the "good old days." I think the great ones are not those who bring about great changes, but those who can meet and adjust to the change that has been made. The coyote's survival, like that of the crow and those exasperating aphids, testifies to an ability to meet change, survive and thrive.

I am not so impressed by the unchanging calm of nature that one reads about all the time, but rather by the constant mutability of nature, and for the elasticity with which wild things face the extremes. Last year it was cold and wet; this year parched and dry. We all talk about it, but the coyote goes about his business. If the streams dry up, all the more stranded fish to fatten him.

And yet the plants and animals are not always responsible mirrors to reflect daily events or normal climates. The knobcone pine is a reflection of a fire-climax. It waits patiently to seed itself, bearing cones that can only be opened in the heat of a fire. That fire may be rare or never come, but it has made that adaptation to an extreme and not the normal. Yet, on the other hand, the trout in this dry summer will die by the thousands in dried-up streams. He is fitted for streams and not ex-streams.

Even the destructive needleminer that's raging through the Tuolumne forest... in its dependence upon the lodgepole pine will it completely destroy its host, and in so doing destroy its own self? We ask these questions. The coyote doesn't. I see him in the meadow. He is scratching his ear and looking down a ground-squirrel hole. I envy his complete immersion in his environment.

Y.N.N., Vol. XXXIX, No. 3, 1960 ✦

About This Story

In a place that went on to pioneer so many ideas that shape our national parks, William L. Neely stood out as one of Yosemite's most famous naturalists. Neely and naturalist Carl Sharsmith offered now-legendary campfire programs at campgrounds in Tuolumne Meadows. Both were the type of naturalists whose unbridled enthusiasm of the natural world infected those who met them. Neely especially was known for being fiercely independent, forging his own conclusions about the environment around him.

Neely's writings were published in *Yosemite Nature Notes*, a monthly journal of the Yosemite Natural History Association. Reading through Neely's "ramblings" allows us to develop our own naturalist's eye, right alongside one of the best.

The Legend of Tu-tok-a-nu'-la

COMPILED BY FRANK LA PENA, CRAIG D. BATES, AND STEVEN P. MEDLEY

Long ago two little bear cubs living in the Valley of Ah-wah'-nee went down to the river to swim. They paddled and splashed about to their hearts' content. The cubs then returned to shore and climbed up on a huge boulder that stood beside the water. They lay down to dry themselves in the warm sunshine, and very soon they fell asleep.

The bear cubs slept so soundly that they did not awaken. Through sleeps, moons and snows, both winter and summer, they slumbered on.

Meanwhile, the great rock upon which they slept began to rise. It rose day and night, little by little, until it had lifted them up high into the sky. In this way the cubs were carried out of sight and beyond voice of their bird and animal friends below. They were lifted up into the blue heavens, far up, far up, until the little bears scraped their faces against the moon. Still they slumbered and slept year after year, safe among the clouds.

The bird and animal people of Ah-wah'-nee missed the bear cubs, and cried for them. One day they all assembled together in the hope of bringing down the little bears from the top of the great rock. One at a time, each animal made a spring up the face of the wall as far as he could leap.

The little mouse could only jump up the breadth of a hand. The rat jumped two handbreadths, and the raccoon made it little further. The grizzly bear made a mighty leap far up the wall, but fell back in vain like all the others. Last of all, the mountain lion tried, and he jumped up further than any other animal. But he, too, fell flat on his back.

Then along come Tul-tak-a-na, an insignificant measuring worm, which even the mouse could crush with his foot. The measuring worm began to creep up the rock. Step by step, a little at a time, he measured his way up. Before long, he was above the mountain lion's jump, and soon he had inched out of sight. In this way the worm crawled up and up through many sleeps for about one whole snow, and at last he reached the top.

Measuring worm picked up the bear cubs and in the same way he went up, took them safely down to the floor of the valley. Since that time, the boulder that grew to be a great high rock has been called Tu-tok-a-nu'-la in honor of Tul-tak-a-na, the measuring worm.

Measuring worm again ascended to the top of the great rock where he leaned out across the Valley of Ah-wah'-nee. He leaned out so far that he stretched across to the opposite side of the canyon with his head on one side and his tail on the other. He then crossed over to the south rim of the valley.

Later he reversed his route, recrossed to the north rim, and again descended to the floor of the valley. The walls of the canyon then began to cave in, and all the bird and animal people of Ah-wah'-nee were forced to flee down the river. In those days, the valley was much deeper than now and somewhat narrower. The caving-in of its walls partly filled the valley and made all of the earth and the piles of rocks that now make up the floor of the valley. ✦

About This Story

Legends explain how our world came to be. This Miwok legend tells us how Tu-tok-a-nu'-la, which you might know as El Capitan, got its name after Tul-tak-a-na, the measuring worm, became the only animal in the forest who could conquer it. So move over Alex Honnold, Tul-tak-a-na was the original free-solo climber.

The challenge in finding native stories is there are so many fabrications that get passed off as authentic. The answer, for us, was to practice decolonization by seeking stories told by native narrators in their own voice. Stories were selected only if they could be traced to American Indian narrators. The book *Legends of the Yosemite Miwok*, published by the Yosemite Association, helped us to find authentic stories and this version of "The Legend of Tu-tok-a-nu'-la" is thought to be one of the first genuine Miwok legends published without embellishment.

Summit Fever

CAROL BLANEY

He called it summit fever
    but I scoffed
        knowing I'm too old for such a malady.

Still
    something strange . . .

I find myself scrambling up boulder-laden ridges,
threading through thick stands of krummholz,
and clinging to feldspar knobs, hanging above sheer drops.

I pray fervently that I might find an easier way down
    that doesn't involve sliding
            off
                the edge.

Surely, this will be the time
    they have to call out search and rescue
    who will find me embarrassed, or dead.
    (My underwear have no holes today, just in case.)

As soon as I make my way down over RV-sized slabs
    and unbalanced stones,
I look up and think: "Well, it wasn't *that* bad. Where else
    can I go?"

And I wonder
  what could explain this
      except some sort of sickness. ✦

About This Story

The majestic granite, stable weather, and easy mountain access made Yosemite the focal point of the rock climbing revolution, with its "Golden Age" between 1955 and 1970, pioneering equipment and techniques that are still used today.

But what to make of the impulse to keep going up and up and up? Poet Carol Blaney offers a humorous take on the "sickness" that has consumed so many of the poor souls who gaze upon the magnificent slabs and stones of Yosemite. Next time you are in the valley, be sure to train your eyes on El Capitan, where you may spot some of these fearless climbers ascending the sheer granite face.

Excerpt from "Among the Animals of the Yosemite"

JOHN MUIR

The Sierra bear, brown or gray, the sequoia of the animals, tramps over all the park, though few travelers have the pleasure of seeing him. On he fares through the majestic forests and cañons, facing all sorts of weather, rejoicing in his strength, everywhere at home, harmonizing with the trees and rocks and shaggy chaparral. Happy fellow! his lines have fallen in pleasant places—lily gardens in silver-fir forests, miles of bushes in endless variety and exuberance of bloom overhill-waves and valleys and along the banks of streams, cañons full of music and waterfalls, parks fair as Eden—places in which one might expect to meet angels rather than bears.

In this happy land no famine comes nigh him. All the year round his bread is sure, for some of the thousand kinds that he likes are always in season and accessible, ranged on the shelves of the mountains like stores in a pantry. From one to another, from climate to climate, up and down he climbs, feasting on each in turn—enjoying as great variety as if he traveled to far-off countries north and south. To him almost every thing is food except granite. Every tree helps to feed him, every bush and herb, with fruits and flowers, leaves and bark; and all the animals he can catch—badgers, gophers, ground squirrels, lizards, snakes, etc., and ants, bees, wasps, old and young, together with their eggs and larvae and nests. Craunched and hashed, down all go to his marvelous stomach, and vanish as if cast into a fire. What digestion! A sheep or a wounded deer or a pig he eats warm, about as quickly as a boy eats a buttered muffin; or should the meat be a month old, it still is welcomed with tremendous relish. After so gross a meal as this, perhaps the next will be strawberries and clover, or raspberries with mushrooms and nuts, or puckery acorns and chokecherries. And as if fearing that anything eatable in all his dominions should escape being eaten, he breaks into cabins to look after sugar, dried apples, bacon, etc. Occasionally he eats the mountaineer's bed; but when he has had a full meal of more tempting dainties he usually leaves it undisturbed, though he has been known to drag it up through a hole in the roof, carry it to the foot of a tree, and lie down on it to enjoy a siesta. Eating everything, never is he himself eaten except by man, and only man is an enemy to be feared. "B'ar meat," said a hunter from whom I was seeking information, "b'ar meat is the best meat in the mountains; their skins make the best beds, and their grease the best butter. Biscuit shortened with b'ar grease goes as far as beans; a man will walk all day on a couple of them biscuit."

In my first interview with a Sierra bear we were frightened and embarrassed, both of us, but the bear's behavior was better than mine. When I discovered him, he was standing in a narrow strip of meadow, and I was concealed behind a tree on the side of it. After studying his appearance as he stood at rest, I rushed toward him to frighten him, that I might study his gait in running. But, contrary to all I had heard about the shyness of bears, he did not run at all; and when I stopped short within a few steps of him, as he held his ground in a fighting attitude, my mistake was monstrously plain. I was then put on my good behavior, and never afterward forgot the right manners of the wilderness.

This happened on my first Sierra excursion in the forest to the north of Yosemite Valley. I was eager to meet the animals, and many of them came to me as if willing to show themselves and make my acquaintance; but the bears kept out of my way.

An old mountaineer, in reply to my questions, told me that bears were very shy, all save grim old grizzlies, and that I might travel the mountains for years without seeing one, unless I gave my mind to them and practiced the stealthy ways of hunters. Nevertheless, it was only a few weeks after I had received this information that I met the one mentioned above, and obtained instruction at first hand.

I was encamped in the woods about a mile back of the rim of Yosemite, beside a stream that falls into the valley by the way of Indian Cañon. Nearly every day for weeks I went to the top of the North Dome to sketch; for it commands a general view of the valley, and I was anxious to draw every tree and rock and waterfall. Carlo, a St. Bernard dog, was my companion,—a fine, intelligent fellow that belonged to a hunter who was compelled to remain all summer on the hot plains, and who loaned him to me for the season for the sake of having him in the mountains, where he would be so much better off. Carlo knew bears through long experience, and he it was who led me to my first interview, though he seemed as much surprised as the bear at my unhunter-like behavior. One morning in June, just as the sunbeams began to stream through the trees, I set out for a day's sketching on the dome; and before we had gone half a mile from camp, Carlo snuffed the air and looked cautiously ahead, lowered his bushy tail, drooped his ears, and began to step softly like a cat, turning every few yards and looking me in the face with a telling expression, saying plainly enough, "There is a bear a little way ahead." I walked carefully in the indicated direction, until I approached a small flowery meadow that I was familiar with and crawled to the foot of a tree on its margin, bearing in mind what I had been told about the shyness of bears. Looking out cautiously over the instep of the tree, I saw a big, burly cinnamon bear about thirty yards off, half erect, his paws resting on the trunk of a fir that had fallen into the meadow, his hips almost buried in grass and flowers. He was listening attentively and trying to catch the scent, showing that in some way he was aware of our approach. I watched his gestures, and tried to make the most of my opportunity to learn what I could about him, fearing he would not stay long. He made a fine picture, standing alert in the sunny garden walled in by the most beautiful firs in the world.

After examining him at leisure, noting the sharp muzzle thrust inquiringly forward, the long shaggy hair on his broad chest, the stiff ears nearly buried in hair, and the slow, heavy way in which he moved his head, I foolishly made a rush on him, throwing up my arms and shouting to frighten him, to see him run. He did not mind the demonstration much; only pushed his head farther forward, and looked at me sharply as if asking, "What now? If you want to fight, I'm ready." Then I began to fear that on me would fall the work of running. But I was afraid to run, lest he should be encouraged to pursue me; therefore I held my ground, staring him in the face within a dozen yards or so, putting on as bold a look as I could, and hoping the influence of the human eye would be as great as it is said to be. Under these strained relations the interview seemed to last a long time. Finally, the bear, seeing how still I was, calmly withdrew his huge paws from the log, gave me a piercing look, as if warning me not to follow him, turned, and walked slowly up the middle of the meadow into the forest; stopping every few steps and looking back to make sure that I was not trying to take him at a disadvantage in a rear attack. I was glad to part with him, and greatly enjoyed the vanishing view as he waded through the lilies and columbines.

Thenceforth I always tried to give bears respectful notice of my approach, and they usually kept well out of my way. Though they often came around my camp in the night, only once afterward, as far as I know, was I very near one of them in daylight. This time it was a grizzly I met; and as luck would have it, I was even nearer to him than I had been to the big cinnamon. Though not a large specimen, he seemed formidable enough at a distance of less than a dozen yards. His shaggy coat was well-grizzled, his head almost white. When I first caught sight of him he was eating acorns under a Kellogg oak, at a distance of perhaps seventy-five yards, and I tried to slip past without disturbing him. But he had either heard my steps on the gravel or caught my scent, for he came straight toward me, stopping every rod or so to look and listen: and as I was afraid to be seen running I crawled on my hands and knees a little way to one side and hid behind a libocedrus, hoping he would pass me unnoticed. He soon came up opposite me, and stood looking ahead, while I looked at him, peering past the bulging trunk of the tree. At last, turning his head, he caught sight of mine, stared sharply a minute or two, and then, with fine dignity, disappeared in a manzanita-covered earthquake talus. ✦

About This Story

No collection of stories from the national parks would be complete without John Muir. This Scottish naturalist published tales combining keen observations with a childlike, and reckless, curiosity. This curiosity often led to adventures like riding an avalanche or climbing a waterfall in search of a better view of the full moon. It was the Yosemite Valley that made Muir's heart flutter, and he returned to it again and again. And it was Muir who, while camped with President Teddy Roosevelt, pitched the idea for an agency that might protect the parks. Today, he's considered by many to be the father of the National Park Service.

"Thousands of tired, nerve-shaken, over-civilized people are beginning to find out that going to the mountains is going home," said Muir. Or, as we find him in this story, said the man running toward the bear to observe its reaction. Luckily for Muir, and for us encountering a black bear while snacking on Sentinel Dome, the bears of Yosemite often prefer to be left alone.

Spring Afternoon, Merced River near the Ahwahnee

GAIL JENSEN SANFORD

I don't have much time. I follow Tenaya Creek
willing to go to Mirror Lake. A shrill vibration of frogs
in the background, the landscape of fledgling pines
and dry marsh converges into the color of deer.
I stop on a dime. The deer is dimly aware, but hungry
for grass. I sink to the ground, then remember my horror
of ticks. She stops and looks around for the sounds, posing,
but my camera is back in my room.

On the path, past the trees, a couple in blue stops to watch.
Another couple, the woman in a red jacket. I wave
slightly, they approach, and kneel by a trunk. He draws
out a camera heavy with lens. Every moment I expect
the deer to flee. One photo, then the need for new
film, and the whirr of machinery. Still, the deer eats.

Ten minutes, five people, one grass-eating deer. I see a pattern
of black dots on her throat, white patches on either side of her tail,
her dun rectangular hide. A half dome of granite above us.
We, the dome, the deer in conjunction like stars
who form a constellation only once in eternity. ✦

About This Story

The story of the national parks is as grand a tale as the lands that they protect. But our love for these lands is built on chance encounters, fleeting visions, and fragile moments. These moments are the ones that inspire a lifelong passion to preserve such special places. Gail Jensen Sanford finds a way to enjoy the moment, to shed the tourists taking pictures, and to savor the constellation of a deer, Half Dome, and herself.

We found this book of poems in the Mariposa Library, the gateway town to Yosemite. For us, two wanderers in search of stories while living out of their car, libraries became important temples of information, and shelter. We learned from the editor of *Yosemite Poets* that this copy was one of the few distributed to the local Yosemite libraries. We're grateful to have happened across this poem, and to have the chance to share it.

Tuolumne Tomboy

SHIRLEY SARGENT

I t didn't take long, maybe half an hour, before I fell towhead over tennis shoes in love with Tuolumne Meadows. I had grown to the advanced age of nine with pine trees on the north rim of the Grand Canyon, pine trees on Mount Charleston in Nevada, and scattered ponderosa conifers around the hadn't-quite-made it resort of Long Barn, California, so it wasn't Tuolumne's forest of scaly-barked lodgepole pines that seduced me. It was more, much more. Awe, soon metamorphosed into love, was inspired by a combination of splendors. It was felt in the cool July breeze; seen in the expansive, river-cut meadows and the domes thrusting boldly into the high blue sky; heard in the sound of rushing water, bird-cry, and breeze; and scented in the pine-needled magic of the Sierra.

My mother, Alice Sargent, my five-year-old sister, Rosalie, and I had just arrived in a camp occupied by several families of Bureau of Public Roads (BPR) engineers, including my dad, Bob Sargent. Friendly women welcomed mother while children inspected us younger interlopers. "The elevation is 8,600 feet here," a woman told mother. "You may want to have your girls rest a while to get used to it."

Simultaneously, but far more quietly, a teenage boy addressed me: "Wanta climb Lembert Dome? Come on." We strolled off, then accelerated as mother called, "Shirley, come back here!" a refrain I was to hear repeatedly during the enchanted summers of 1936 and 1937, summers that merge into one in memory.

Instead of resting on a cot in a tent, I acclimatized myself by scrambling up a steep trail and climbing a granite ridge to the top of Lembert Dome, several hundred feet above the meadows. My leader, Glendon, was offhand when I tried to articulate my wonder at the view, but he pointed out the singular grandeur of

192

Cathedral and Unicorn peaks to the southwest and Mount Dana, Mount Gibbs, and Mammoth Peak to the east. My lifelong love affair with Tuolumne Meadows—with all of Yosemite National Park—had begun.

What is still remembered as the Great Depression, and the government's efforts to put thousands of men back to work by allocating millions of dollars for highway and bridge construction in National Parks, Forests, and Monuments, was responsible for our being in the high heaven of Tuolumne Meadows. The BPR staff were present, surveying and inspecting the construction progress on a modern highway to replace the narrow, wandering pioneer Tioga Road. My handsome engineer dad was participating in making Yosemite history at the same time as he was keeping his family in beans and bread.

Our BPR camp was already historic—for the irregular rows of tent frames and such amenities as a bathhouse and grease rack that had been built and occupied by the Civilian Conservation Corps (CCC) boys earlier in the thirties—and would later become a summer home for entomologists and various ranger-naturalists. Only the messhall's L-shaped floor was left, but it had been recycled into a platform for Saturday night dances. My parents and other BPR couples circled it, accompanied by band music from car radios. Headlights supplied lighting. Camp kids—there were four or five of us besides the teenager—utilized the flooring for less romantic but eminently satisfactory pursuits such as hopping, jumping rope, and playing with toy cars.

Besides the camp and another larger one a couple of miles to the southwest, the CCC men had constructed the 300-site Tuolumne Meadows campground, which featured granite-rocked, shake-roofed restrooms with inside plumbing—grandeur in the wilds. Our camp had out houses, but the elegant bathhouse with showers and laundry tubs gave great comfort to cleanliness-minded adults.

Seymour Coffman was resident engineer of the job. His wife soon allied with mother, and their little girl and my sister became inseparable. Glendon's parents were Georgie and Frank Swan. A childless couple named Jack and Pat Kiefer impressed me because they drove clear to Bishop for Sunday Mass. "Fibber" Kenny and his parents, Mary and Lee Storch, and the three Ciceros, were the people I remember best. I'll never forget Carmen Cicero because her exuberant yodels resounded and echoed beautifully through the camp.

But, instead of yodeling, she screamed in the shower when she found the missing and mourned diamond from Mrs. Kiefer's wedding ring. "All the women came running," Carmen recalled, "and Pat nearly fainted. When Jack came home, he was so thankful he drove the long, twisty miles to Lee Vining and bought me a case of beer."

The public campground, constructed in anticipation of an increase in visitation once the new road was finished, had opened barely a month before we arrived. Campers were entertained at night by campfire programs put on by an ardent and popular young ranger-naturalist named Carl Sharsmith. It would be pleasant to say that, at age nine, I fell under his influence, as I did years later—but not in 1936. However, I had my first lessons in conservation that summer. My "teacher" was not a naturalist but a ranger on the protective staff, then in charge of the Tuolumne Meadows District. His name was Duane Jacobs, and he epitomized the public image of a ranger: tall, handsome, broad-shouldered, quiet-spoken, yet commanding.

I first saw him the morning after we moved into our tent, when he informed Mom why we couldn't keep our cat at Tuolumne. Cats, he said politely, were disruptive if not fatal to wildlife. Our tail-swishing Persian was already on a leash, but mom promised to cage her and send her off via Greyhound bus as soon as possible. My petless aunt and uncle in the desert town of Palmdale agreed to provide her with temporary refuge.

My next encounter with ranger Jacobs was more personal, Dad had made me a slingshot, and I was off in the woods, ineffectually aiming pebbles at a chattering crested jay that, the ranger must have realized, was absolutely safe. Nevertheless, he introduced me to the idea of the fragility of birds and small mammals, for we were being scolded by what I knew as a "picket pin," but which he identified as a Belding ground squirrel.

"Wouldn't it be a shame," he concluded, "if you hurt or killed that pretty bird?"

Not once had he raised his voice or suggested confiscating my weapon, but he left me imbued with a protective zeal that sent me running up the trail onto the granite backbone of Lembert Dome. There, winded but still purposeful, I flung my slingshot off into space—and was immediately sorry. But a childish grasp of preservation, which later expanded, was implanted in my tomboy self.

Our camp was on a sloping mountainside, between but out of sight of both the old and new Tioga roads. Dad set off to work soon after sunlight slanted through the pines, and Mom spent the days working over our two-burner Coleman stove, washing dishes, or performing myriad mundane tasks. Mom and Dad's double bed, bunk beds (mine was the top one), a makeshift closet, and pieces of "Hercules mahogany" furnished the adjoining sleeping tent. Strong wooden powder boxes, originally made by the Hercules Powder Company for storing dynamite, were prized because they could be transformed into cupboards, chests, stools, and even chairs.

At night Dad hoisted our cooler, or bear baffle, high in the air to keep food away from bears. Actually, these animals were rarely in our camp. "You and Rosalie used to go with us," Carmen wrote me, "to see the bears at the garbage dump. Some of them were huge. We had a small bear climb a tree in back of the bathhouse once. But our biggest worry was the mice. The minute we extinguished the gas lantern at night, they were scampering all over."

Our screen-sided, canvas-covered "front" room contained a sink with running water, the Coleman stove, a wood-devouring airtight stove, a wood box that I was supposed to help fill, a picnic table, and more pieces of Hercules mahogany. Rosalie was content with playing dolls inside, but I was happier out of the tent's confines and away from mother's admonitions that the wood box needed filling or the broom needed wielding. After breakfast I would escape to the outhouse, and from there take off for hours of freedom. Carmen remembers me as "always on the go, looking for new places to explore."

Often I perched on top of a steep, triangular-sided boulder just off the shoulder of the new road, carefully writing down the numbers affixed to dump trucks, road graders, and steam shovels. No doubt amused at my industry, drivers would wave. Further delight was supplied by the times when my sister found me but could not climb up to join me.

Since electrification was far in the future, the only item on ice in our camp was beer. Bottles were kept in a snow-filled washtub, replenished a couple of times a week from slow-melting drifts near Tioga Pass. The inviting tub was kept in the shade of pines on the slope above our tent. Anticipating a clandestine tasting session, Dad gave me a bottle to try. A hearty swallow instantly forestalled youthful addiction.

Another recreational feature of camp life was a horseshoe pit near our tent. The clunk and thud of horseshoes were accompanied by masculine shouts of "Anybody can see that's a leaner!" Such comments and spirited arguments coincided with the squeals of whichever delighted youngster was being pushed high in the tire swing by a man awaiting his turn at horseshoes.

On weekdays at least two of the women—Mom being one—drove down to the meadow, where radio reception was clear enough to hear "Stella Dallas" and "Mary Marlin." Rosalie was still so young she took naps, and she would curl up on the back seat. I was supposed to stay in camp, but more likely I was out in the woods or along the Dana Fork of the Tuolumne River, forbidden territory which, Mom warned, "you could drown in." That was possible, but there were many safe places to wade across to the other side. Often I was followed by Fibber Kenny, a six-year-old who loved both to fish and prevaricate.

One time he tagged along and witnessed my tumble into the water. I remember undressing except for my underpants, leaving my clothes on a boulder to dry, and wandering off with Kenny's "wait for me" plaint his sole reaction.

The grass was greener and thicker on the other side of the river. Furthermore there were few observers—perhaps an occasional fisherman or two—whereas there were cars, drivers, and admonitory adults on the camp side. Once, while I was lacing my shoes after a crossing with them held in my hands, one fell in the river and was swept away. Catastrophe! Not only would Mother know that I had disobeyed her, but I had only one other pair of shoes—school shoes. The word "Depression" meant little to me except that we couldn't afford anything extra. That had been brought forcibly home to me after I had carelessly dropped our sole flashlight down an outhouse hole. If flashlights were essential and expensive, then shoes, I realized, must be even more so.

After work, Dad and I hunted for the missing tennis shoe, which, fortunately, he found—thoroughly waterlogged. My parents were neither tyrannical nor penurious, just scraping by on about one hundred dollars a month. "You girls and your mother," Carmen Cicero said, "often went to Lee Vining with us to buy groceries. We tried to get by on a dollar a day for food."

My next misadventure in the Dana Fork involved a rock cutting a bare toe. I howled loudly enough so that Carmen alerted Mother: "Alice, I think Shirley is drowning." My Mom's unflappable reply, repeated to me later, was, "She wouldn't be making that much noise if she was drowning." Retribution for that episode was worse than a spanking, for Mom cleaned out the wound with a liberal application of smelly, stinging iodine. Iodine, castor oil, and, it seemed to me, spankings, were Mom's remedies for any and all physical and behavioral problems. Fortunately praise and hugs were also given freely.

Thunder, lightning, and pouring rain were a frequent afternoon diversion. Our tent leaked, and Mom developed a rating system for a storm's severity. A two- or three-pan storm with the accompanying sound of plunks and drips was easily controllable, but an eight-pan and once even a ten-pan rain overtaxed her supply of utensils. I enjoyed dumping pans into a bucket, and was exhilarated by the fast-moving storms and warmed by the airtight stove and mugs of cocoa.

One memorable day I was caught out in the woods by a storm, and quickly soaked. I frantically sought shelter, and found a small cave somewhere in the vicinity of Puppy Dome. While I shivered, teeth chattering, I glanced around in the gloom, and discerned rude but colorful stick figures—Indian pictographs. I was awed, and planned to bring my family to see them, but I never could relocate the place.

Being sent on an errand to the store down the old road was always a joy. Since Puppy Dome was just across a meadow from the large, long tent that housed food, camping equipment, fishing supplies, and some clothes, a quick climb and a few moments to savor the view from the top prefaced my trip. After buying whatever mother needed, I would become mesmerized by a tantalizing display of rubber and leather boots shelved at the back of the store. I had studied them frequently, and had decided on a pair of ankle-high, laced leather boots as essential to my well-being. No other boots, either in the store or in the indispensable wish-books—"Sears 'n Sawbucks" and "Monkey Wards" catalogs—could possibly carry me up to a mountaintop more comfortably and speedily than they.

Of course my parents were acutely aware of my obsession, but when the glad day came that I really was to climb a mountain, I wore my badly worn tennis shoes. New ones had been ordered but had not yet arrived. Glendon, his father, Dad, and I drove to a parking lot near Tioga Pass, then took off across the flowery, somewhat boggy meadow toward Mount Dana, towering above us, red and rocky, at 13,053 feet. The fact that the elevation of Tioga Pass, our starting point, was 9,945 feet did not diminish my exultation: I was going to climb a 13,000-foot peak!

Dad had warned me that I was not to complain, and, though frequently breathless and weary, I didn't. Near the top, however, rocks cut through the sole on one shoe, and I asked him to carry me. "No way" was not a common expression then, but his response was negative. He and the others left me behind. It was so quiet that I could hear water from melting snow gurgling under the jumble of rocks. Slowly, gingerly, I limped after them, trying to keep the torn shoe from touching the sharpest rocks.

By the time I reached the top, the tear and the discomfort had grown considerably, but were instantly dismissed in wonder at the vistas.

Above, the azure sky formed a dazzling arc, encircling me was infinity, and below was color, in green meadows, the blue glints of ponds, and expanses of lakes. Dad pointed out Mono Lake on the east, beyond which, he told me, was high desert and Nevada. He swiveled to point out the familiar dominant peaks to the west: Cathedral, Unicorn, Cockscomb. I identified Lembert Dome, but its stature, hitherto so impressive, seemed reduced.

In that array of beauty and might, amid surroundings of unimaginable natural grandeur, I felt awed, enriched, and humble. In many ways, that climb to the summit of Dana was the high point of my childhood.

When we arrived back at camp I was limping, both shoe soles flapping and a stocking cut through, but still I was exhilarated and inspired. Dad said proudly, "Here's a hiker who deserves a pair of boots." Mom's response was less positive. "Maybe for Christmas, but just look at what came in today's mail." New blue tennis shoes that looked, and felt, wonderful. ✦

About This Story

Shirley Sargent is a preeminent historian of Yosemite. From her home in Foresta, a community within the park's boundaries, she recorded the history of early settlers, the Ahwahnee and Wawona Hotels, and many aspects of early Yosemite life through her numerous books. But this essay is not a historical document. It's a memoir on a childhood summer spent peak bagging, as her father helped rebuild Tioga Road.

This recollection is more poignant if you know that a rare crippling disease would relegate Sargent to a wheelchair for the rest of her life. Her love of climbing brings her story to life, and her memories from early childhood as a Yosemite tomboy were some of her most treasured.

YELLOWSTONE NATIONAL PARK

A Storied Wonderland

OUR NATION'S very first national park and
still one of the most visited, Yellowstone
National Park was initially protected
for its thermal features. Its abundant
wildlife, geysers, hot springs, and sweeping
landscapes are truly stunning, and leave
you wondering if you've accidentally
traveled to another planet.

illustration by
ZOE KELLER

Yellowstone National Park, we were told, chooses her own. So many personal stories begin with a summer job or visit. Then, curiosity, awe, and the wonder of Yellowstone sets in. A summer job turns into a permanent home. Once you're chosen, you don't get away. And why would you want to? The people we spoke to live and work here because they feel a calling to be here.

That's the power of Yellowstone. Here is the first place that the country ever called a national park—a status that elevates all conversations about it. People come from all over the world to see, not just a geyser, but an icon: Old Faithful. They come to watch the wolves, the bears, and the bison, all brought back from the brink of extinction. These are, yes, icons of conservation, but also of the West. And all that extra attention means every incident is public, every decision scrutinized. Anything can become a controversy. In Yellowstone, more than any other park we visited, the press office works diligently to manage its message. In most parks, we were able to reach out directly to rangers and affiliated groups. In Yellowstone, those requests were directed toward the press office, who tracked us down by phone, email, and Facebook, to ask that we speak to them immediately. As the symbol of the national park system, and the American West, Yellowstone receives all the glory, and all the blame.

A number of incidents at Yellowstone made national news the summer of our visit. There was the visitor who loaded a stray bison calf into his van, thinking he was saving its life (he wasn't, and the calf ended up needing to be humanely euthanized). There was the visitor who fell into an acidic hot spring after straying off the boardwalk, and whose body couldn't be recovered. There was the woman who was tossed into the air after trying to take a selfie with a bison. Incidents like these can occur in any national park, but they're more visible in Yellowstone. We worried that by the time we reached the park, they would no longer be allowing wild humans in.

For Yellowstone, with its sulfurous stenches and belching mud pits, beautiful isn't the right word. At the time of Yellowstone's founding, Lewis Carroll's *Alice's Adventures in Wonderland* was a national phenomenon. In the book, Alice crawls through a rabbit hole, and finds herself in a fantasy world full of spectacular creatures. Described by its indescribability, Yellowstone captured the attention of a young nation, and earned a new nickname: Wonderland.

Two things happen when you watch tourists at Yellowstone today: they stare in disbelief, then they pull out their cameras for a picture. It's as if they instinctively know the feeling shared by the first explorers to Yellowstone. The landscape was too unlike any other landscape—almost like being on a foreign planet—and no words could do it justice. It took three major scientific expeditions before the rest of the country believed their accounts. Upon receiving an early account of the geyser basins, *Lippincott's Magazine* responded, "We don't print fiction." In other words, pics or it didn't happen.

Yellowstone sits atop an active supervolcano that is responsible for all the park's thermal features. Although the last eruption occurred 70,000 years ago, magma still sits below the surface, only three miles below in some places. This magma warms any water that seeps underground, turning it into gas. Over time, the gas builds pressure until it bubbles, steams, and bursts back out of the earth to the delight of visitors. Over half of the world's geysers can be found in Yellowstone.

Unlike other national parks across the country, we found almost none of the typical native creation myths, although we found many accounts of encounters with natives. This lack of native stories reflects the complex histories Yellowstone had with its native inhabitants. Early park superintendents mused that Indians were afraid of the geysers. With twenty-six contemporary tribes claiming a connection to park lands, we know that Yellowstone was an important place for American Indians, a pilgrimage site for gathering materials or performing ceremonies. Contemporary historians agree the "fear" story was a myth. Instead, historians suggest that natives may have deliberately stayed quiet about Yellowstone. By the time the Yellowstone expeditions (1869–1871) took place, native tribes were at war with European settlers. At stake was ownership of the land, and the future of the way entire nations would relate to the earth. We had the pleasure of sitting fireside with a Lakota family, visiting to teach a multiday course about native medicine and storytelling, who expressed their happiness at seeing the park preserved, but also a bittersweet feeling whenever they visit.

Today, grizzlies, black bears, elk, moose, antelope, sheep, bison, wolves, and bald eagles all call Yellowstone home. While the thermal features may have inspired its preservation, many believe that the opportunity to see and study wildlife is the premier feature of the park today. But wildlife management evolves constantly. Superintendent Horace Albright, who would become the Park Service's second director, believed Yellowstone's role was to present tame wildlife for all to enjoy—"aesthetic conservation." Under this policy, wolves were removed in the early 1900s. A US military policy of "kill the buffalo, kill the Indian" reduced a bison population estimated at 30 million to less than 400 wild bison by 1893, leaving an apocalyptic landscape of skulls and bones in its wake. Yellowstone's rivers were then stocked with game fish, challenging native species for their habitat. And, after abruptly ending the practice of feeding food waste to grizzlies, the park service had to eliminate all the wild bears that associated humans with food. This practice reduced the population to 136 bears by 1975, making them an endangered species. Parks today have shifted to "nature-oriented" preservation, and animal populations have made a comeback. Yellowstone's 7,500 bison are now the world's largest free-ranging bison population. The grizzly population has risen to 700, and 104 wolves roam in 11 packs. Any of these animals alone could be a symbol of the American West. Together, they represent a wilderness gone by, and the source of unending traffic jams.

Many of the established megafauna populations create modern-day conflicts around the park. For local ranchers, wild animals are a challenge to their livelihoods. Half of Yellowstone's bison population carries brucellosis, a disease that can spread to cattle. As a result, the Interagency Bison Management Program controls the populations of the Yellowstone bison: a nice way of saying wild bison can be in the wrong place, at the wrong time. And as grizzly bear populations recover, soon to be delisted from the Endangered Species Act, heated arguments are picking up about who has the right to hunt these animals.

To manage all this wildness, the park offers a litany of warnings to visitors. Any large mammals, even elk, will attack, so please stay twenty-five to one hundred yards away. Thermal features, although beautiful, are fragile and unpredictable, so please stay on the boardwalks. Bears will attack if startled, so please hike in groups of three or more, make a lot of noise, and always carry bear spray. In this place, where humans are not at the top of the food chain, it's safety over solitude. Now in the second trimester of our pregnancy, these dangers and threats made us avoid the more adventurous hikes. Instead, we found ourselves among the crowds, ooh-ing at geysers like Old Faithful and aah-ing at hot springs like the

Morning Glory Pool. While we encountered busloads of tourists at every park, the sensitivity of Yellowstone's landscape, and the way it crams visitors onto narrow boardwalks, made it feel even more crowded.

This was the last park of our road trip, a journey of discovery into the heart of who and what makes each national park unique. After a relatively careful summer of travel, we were hit by road-trip woes all at once. Driving through the Lamar Valley, we caught a nasty pothole that blew out two tires, hundreds of miles from any gas station on a Sunday, during a thunderstorm, and only a few hundred feet from wild bison. Three days before we headed home, our tent broke for good. To protect ourselves from Yellowstone's unpredictable weather, we had to drive two hours to Bozeman to replace the tent that had been home for our entire trip.

We ended our journey at the beginning: the first national park in the country, which still stands as a symbol for the national park system. All of Yellowstone's icons inspire pilgrimage, but two major sites convey the dual roles of this important park. There's Old Faithful, the most famous of all the landscape features, attracting attention and visitors worldwide. When Yellowstone was first created, it erupted up to 8,400 gallons of boiling water to a height of 185 feet every sixty minutes—the geyser you could set your watch to (although it spouts every ninety minutes today). And Roosevelt Arch, where Teddy Roosevelt dedicated the first park, and set into motion the idea of a land, preserved and owned by all the citizens of the country.

Yellowstone

E. M. CARPENTER

Golden summer sunshine days, in high Wyoming lands,
 Air of spruce and pine and snowy breezes mingle
In the freshness of a western morn, the glory of a mountain day.
Winding trails in sylvan beauty unfold a vista of rare sights:
Round wooded slopes, thru flower bespangled vales,
Where the yellow columbine and purple violet dance
In the summer breezes, and reflect the perfume of a mountain shower.
Shy orchids in primeval forests peep slyly from out their hidden dells,
Undisturbed by the stealthy coyote or the wild bear's padded tread.
White crested roaring torrents leap o'er boulders arched by giant
 trees,
And the wary rainbow trout lurks in the eddying pools.
Towering timbered heights, forest infinite, merging into valleys,
With emerald gem lakes in their restful settings of vivid green.
Mighty rivers of crystal blue on their journey to the sea
Break o'er dizzy heights, and plunge into a labyrinth of painted canyons.
Giant birds circle in the chasm, diving and splashing thru the rainbow
 mists.
Like the swell of rare music, come the breezes thru the
Lofty spruce tree avenues shadowing sunlight and shade,
And from the cabin fireplace floats out upon the forest
Laden air, like incense, the scent of burning pinewood.
Old Faithful growls its subterranean thunder and spouts

A clear green column of water in this wonderland of dreams.

Transparent lakes mirror the matchless blue, picturing in their placid
surface

Mountain ranges and fantastic peaks of weird grandeur.

The elk ambles cautiously from out the aspen grove, hides her

Fawn in the tall grass, and stands in silhouette against the somber
wood.

The spell of the quiet nightfall and evening shower is

Heavy with the scent of pine and sage bush.

The closing day with waning sun glimmers slowly down

The west and fades into evening twilight's shadows,

And overhead the myriad starlit sky. Moon-beam flashing streams

Echo thru the solitude enchanting beauty of a summer night.

Yellowstone, old Yellowstone, in dreamland fancies ne'er forgot,

And twilight memories fondly linger round old earth's most favored
spot. ✦

About This Story

Golden summer sunshine days, perfume of a mountain shower, and forest infinite, merging into valleys—the words of Carpenter's "Yellowstone" perfectly captured the smells, sights, and sounds of the park we were engrossed in.

We discovered this poem in the vast archives of the Yellowstone Research Library, which collects any and all published and unpublished materials related to Yellowstone. Even a poem like "Yellowstone," published in the November-December 1943 issue of *New Age*, and for which we and other scholars have found no other information about the publication or the author, has a home here. Two full days in the library, and we had only scratched the surface of the collection. But those two days helped us uncover some wonderful writings, such as this evocative poem.

Yellowstone Park and How It Was Named

WILLIAM TOD HELMUTH

The Devil was sitting in Hades one day,
In a very disconsolate sort of a way.
One could tell from his vigorous switching of tail,
His scratching his horn with the point of his nail,
That something had gone with His Majesty wrong,
The steam was so thick and the sulphur so strong.
He rose from his throne with a gleam in his eye,
And beckoning an agate-eyed imp standing by,
Commanded forthwith to be sent to him there
Old Charon, employed in collecting the fare
Of the wicked, who crossed the waters of Styx,
And found themselves soon in a deuce of a fix.
Old Charon, thus summoned, came soon to his chief,
As the devil was angry, the confab was brief.
Said the Devil to Charon, "Now, what shall I do?
The world it grows old and grows wickeder, too;
From Portland, Chicago, Francisco, New York,
I get in my mortals too fast for my fork;
I haven't the room in these caverns below,
St. Peter above is rejecting them so.
So hie you, my Charon, to earth, right away.
Fly over the globe without any delay,

And find me a spot quite secluded and drear,
Where I can drill holes from the center in here.
I must blast out more space; so survey the spot well
For the project on hand is [the] enlargement of Hell.
But recollect one thing, Old Charon, when you
Can locate the district where I can bore through,
There must be conveniences scattered around
To carry on business when I'm above ground.
An 'ink pot' must always be ready at hand
To write out the names of the parties I strand.
There must be a 'punch bowl,' a 'frying pan,' too,
A 'cauldron' in which to concoct a ragout.
An 'old faithful' sentinel showing my power
Must shoot a salute on the earth every hour,
And should any mortal by accident view
The spot you have chosen, why, this you must do:
Develop a series of pools, green and blue,
That while these poor earthlings may beauties admire
They'll forget that below I'm poking the fire.
Now fly away, Charon, be quick as you can,
For my place here's so full that I can't roast a man."
To earth flew fleet Charon, to regions of ice;
He found these too cold—so away in a trice
He sought a location in Africa's sands,
Prospecting and finding too much on his hands
He sought out Australia—Siberia, too, [and]
The north part of China—no! they would not do;
Till just as about to relinquish the chase
He stumbled upon a miraculous place.
'Twas deep in the midst of a mountainous range,
Surrounded by valleys secluded and strange,
In a country the greatest, the grandest, the best
To be found upon Earth—America's West.

Here the crust seemed quite thin, the purified air
With the chemicals hidden around everywhere,
Would soon make the lakes that the Devil desired.
He flew to Chicago and there to him wired:
"I've found you a place never looked at before;
You may heat up the rocks, turn on water, and bore."

The Devil with mortals kept plying the fire,
Extracting the water around from the mire,
And boring great holes with a terrible dust,
Till soon quite a number appeared in the crust.
Then he turned on the steam—lo! upward did fly,
Through rents in the surface, the rocks to the sky.
Then with a rumble there came from each spot
Huge volumes of water remarkably hot,
That had been there in caverns since Lucifer fell—
Thus immensely enlarging the confines of Hell,
And it happens that *now* when Old Charon brings in
A remarkable load of original sin,
That His Majesty quietly rakes up the coals,
And up spouts the water, in jets, through the holes,
One may tell by the number of spurts when they come,
How many poor mortals the Devil takes home.

But Yankees can sometimes, without doing evil,
O'ermatch in sagacity even the Devil.
For not long ago Uncle Sam came that way
And said to himself, "Here's the Devil to pay.
Successful I've been in all previous wars;
Now Satan shall bow to the Stripes and the Stars.
This property's mine, and I hold it in fee,
And all of this earth shall its majesty see.
The deer and the elk unmolested shall roam,

The bear and the buffalo each have a home;
The eagle shall spring from her ayrie and soar
O'er crags in the canyons where cataracts roar;
The wild fowls shall circle the pools in their flight,
The geysers shall flash in the moonbeams at night,
Now I christen the country—let all nations hark—
I name it the *Yellowstone National Park*." ✦

About This Story

Yellowstone is a wondrous place where the earth opens up to reveal boiling mud, sulfurous stenches, and erupting geysers. It was a landscape that captured the imagination of an America expanding west, and played a key role in establishing the National Park Service. In this poem, William Tod Helmuth imagines how such a wondrous place as Yellowstone was discovered.

Early travelers visited by train or horse-drawn carriage, and only the very wealthy could afford the expense of a three to four week Yellowstone vacation. As a doctor who dabbled in poetry, Helmuth was part of a group of visitors who fed the growing national curiosity about Yellowstone with accounts of their travels. The poem appeared in booklets published by Jack Haynes, the park's official photographer. Helmuth's playful account imagines Yellowstone as a whim of the Devil, seeking a home on earth with cauldrons, ink pots, and frying pans. After searching all over the world, Charon manages to find only one place sufficiently monstrous: Yellowstone.

Excerpts from
"Thirty-Seven Days of Peril"

TRUMAN EVERTS

n the day that I found myself separated from the company, our course was impeded by the dense growth of the pine forest. Large tracts of fallen timber frequently rendered our progress almost impossible. Whenever we came to one of these immense windfalls, each man engaged in the pursuit of a passage through it. With the idea that I had found one, I strayed out of sight and hearing of my comrades. As separations like this frequently occurred, it gave me no alarm.

I rode on in the direction, which I supposed had been taken, until darkness overtook me in the dense forest. This was disagreeable enough, but caused me no alarm. I had no doubt of being with the party at breakfast the next morning. I selected a spot for comfortable repose, picketed my horse, built a fire, and went to sleep.

The next morning I rose at early dawn, saddled and mounted my horse, and took my course in the supposed direction of the camp. In searching for the trail I became somewhat confused. The falling foliage of the pines had obliterated every trace of travel. I was obliged frequently to dismount and examine the ground for the faintest indications.

Coming to an opening, from which I could see several vistas, I dismounted for the purpose of selecting one leading in the direction I had chosen. Leaving my horse unhitched, I walked a few rods into the forest. While I was surveying the ground my horse took fright, and I turned around in time to see him disappearing at full speed among the trees. That was the last I ever saw of him. My blankets, gun, pistols, fishing tackle, matches—everything, except the clothing on my person, a couple of knives, and a small opera-glass—were attached to the saddle.

I did not yet realize the possibility of a permanent separation from the company. Instead of following up the pursuit of their camp, I engaged in an effort to recover my horse. Half a day's search convinced me of its impracticability.

As the day wore on without any discovery, alarm took the place of anxiety at the prospect of another night alone in the wilderness—this time without food or fire. But even this dismal foreboding was cheered by the hope that I should soon rejoin my companions, who would laugh at my adventure and incorporate it as a thrilling episode into the journal of our trip.

At no time during my period of exile did I experience so much mental suffering from the cravings of hunger as when, exhausted with this long day of fruitless search, I resigned myself to a couch of pine foliage. The forest seemed alive with the screeching of night birds, the angry barking of coyotes, and the prolonged, dismal howl of the gray wolf. These sounds were full of terror, and drove slumber from my eyelids.

Early the next morning I rose unrefreshed. For the first time, I realized that I was lost. Then came a crushing sense of destitution. No food, no fire; no means to procure either; alone in an unexplored wilderness, one hundred and fifty miles from the nearest human abode, surrounded by wild beasts, and famishing with hunger. It was no time for despondency. A moment afterwards I felt how calamity can elevate the mind, in the formation of the resolution "not to perish in that wilderness."

Night was fast approaching, and darkness would come with it. While looking for a spot where I might repose in safety, my attention was attracted to a small green plant of so lively a hue as to form a striking contrast with the deep pine foliage. I pulled it up by the root, which was long and tapering, not unlike a radish. It was a thistle. I tasted it; it was palatable and nutritious. My appetite craved it, and the first meal in four days was made on thistle-roots. Eureka! I had found food.

Overjoyed at this discovery, with hunger allayed, I stretched myself under a tree and fell asleep. How long I slept I know not; but suddenly I was roused by a loud, shrill scream, like that of a human being in distress, poured, seemingly, into the very portals of my ear. There was no mistaking that fearful voice. It was the screech of a mountain lion, so alarmingly near as to cause every nerve to thrill with terror.

I seized with convulsive grasp the limbs of the friendly tree, and swung myself into it. Scrambling hurriedly from limb to limb, I was soon as near the top as safety would permit. The savage beast was snuffing and growling below, apparently on the very spot I had just abandoned.

I answered every growl with a responsive scream. Terrified at the pawing of the beast, I increased my voice to its utmost volume, broke branches from the limbs, and madly hurled them at the spot whence the continued howlings proceeded.

The animal now began to circle the tree, as if to select a spot for springing into it. I shook, with a strength increased by terror, the slender trunk until every limb rustled with the motion. All in vain. The terrible creature pursued his walk around the tree, lashing the ground with his tail, and prolonging his howlings almost to a roar. It was too dark to see, but the movements of the lion kept me apprised of its position.

Whenever I heard it on one side of the tree I speedily changed to the opposite. I would alternately sweat and thrill with horror at the thought of being torn to pieces and devoured by this formidable monster. Expecting at every moment that it would take the deadly leap, I tried to collect my thoughts. Just at this moment it occurred to me that I would try silence.

Clasping the trunk of the tree with both arms, I sat perfectly still. The lion, still filling the forest with the echo of his howlings, suddenly imitated my example. This silence was more terrible than the clatter and crash of his movements through the brushwood. Now I did not know from what direction to expect his attack. Moments passed like hours. After a lapse of time that I cannot estimate, the beast gave a spring into the thicket and ran screaming into the forest.

Had strength permitted, I should have retained my perch till daylight. But with escape from the jaws of the ferocious brute came a sense of overpowering weakness which almost palsied me. Incredible as it may seem, I lay down in my old bed and was soon lost in a slumber.

I did not awake until after daylight. One of those dreary storms of mingled snow and rain, common to these high latitudes, had set in. My clothing, which had been much torn, exposed my person to its "pitiless peltings."

I knew that my escape from the wilderness must be accomplished, if at all, by my own unaided exertions. This thought was terribly afflicting, and brought before me, in vivid array, all the dreadful realities of my condition. I could see no ray of hope. In this condition of mind I could find no better shelter than the spreading branches of a spruce tree, under which, covered with earth and boughs, I lay during the two succeeding days; the storm, meanwhile, raging with unabated violence.

Nothing gave me more concern than the want of fire. I recalled everything I had ever read or heard of the means by which fire could be produced; but none of them were within my reach. An escape without it was simply impossible.

As I lay in my bower, anxiously awaiting the disappearance of the snow, it occurred to me that I would erect some sort of monument, which might, at some future day, inform a casual visitor of the circumstances under which I had perished. At that moment a gleam of sunshine lit up the bosom of the lake, and with it the thought flashed upon my mind that I could, with a lens from my opera glasses, get fire from heaven. Oh, happy, life-renewing thought!

Instantly subjecting it to the test of experiment when I saw the smoke curl from the bit of dry wood in my fingers, I felt, if the whole world were offered me for it, I would cast it aside before parting with that little spark. I was now the happy possessor of food and fire. These would carry me through. I said to myself, "I will not despair."

My stay at the springs was prolonged several days by an accident that befell me on the third night after my arrival there. An unlucky movement while asleep broke the crust on which I reposed, and the hot steam, pouring upon my hip, scalded it severely before I could escape. This new affliction, added to my frost-bitten feet, already festering, was the cause of frequent delay and unceasing pain through all my wanderings.

All that day I traveled over timber heaps, amid treetops, and through thickets. At noon I took the precaution to obtain fire. With a brand, which I kept alive by frequent blowing and constant waving to and fro, at a late hour in the afternoon, faint and exhausted, I kindled a fire for the night on the only vacant spot I could find amid a dense wilderness of pines. The deep gloom of the forest, in the spectral light revealed on all sides of me a compact and unending growth of trunks, and an impervious canopy of somber foliage; the shrieking of night-birds; the supernaturally human scream of the mountain lion; the prolonged howl of the wolf, made me insensible to all other forms of suffering.

A bright and glorious morning succeeded the dismal night, and brought with it the conviction that I had been the victim of uncontrollable nervous excitement. I resolved henceforth to banish it altogether, and resumed my journey towards the lake.

I doubt if distress and suffering can ever entirely obliterate all sense of natural grandeur and magnificence. Lost in the wonder and admirations inspired by this vast world of beauties, I nearly forgot to improve the few moments of remaining sunshine to obtain fire. With a lighted brand in my hand, I effected a most difficult and arduous descent of the abrupt and stony headland to the beach of the lake.

An hour of sunshine in the afternoon enabled me to procure fire, which, in the usual manner, I carried to my camping place. There I built a fire, and to protect myself from the wind, which was blowing violently, lashing the lake into foam, I made a bower of pine boughs, crept under it, and very soon fell asleep.

How long I slept I know not, but I was aroused by the snapping and cracking of the burning foliage, to find my shelter and the adjacent forest in a broad sheet of flame. My left hand was badly burned, and my hair singed closer than a barber would have trimmed it, while I made my escape from the semicircle of burning trees. Among the disasters of this fire, there was none I felt more seriously than the loss of my buckle-tongue knife, my pin fishhook, and tape fish line.

The grandeur of the burning forest surpasses description. An immense sheet of flame, following to their tops the lofty trees of an almost impenetrable pine forest, leaping madly from top to top, and sending thousands of forked tongues a hundred feet or more. Favored by the gale, the conflagration spread with lightning swiftness over an illimitable extent of country—leaving a broad and blackened trail of spectral trunks shorn of limbs and foliage, smoking and burning, to mark the immense sweep of its devastation.

While I was thus considering whether to remain and search for a passage or return to the Yellowstone, I experienced one of those strange hallucinations which many of my friends have misnamed insanity, but which to me was Providence. An old clerical friend, for whose character and counsel I had always cherished peculiar regard, in some unaccountable manner seemed to be standing before me, charged with advice which would relieve my perplexity. I seemed to hear him say, as if in a voice and with the manner of authority, "Go back immediately, as rapidly as your strength will permit. There is no food here, and the idea of scaling these rocks is madness."

"Doctor," I rejoined, "the distance is too great. I cannot live to travel it."

"Say not so. Your life depends upon the effort. Return at once. Start now, lest your resolution falter. Travel as fast and as far as possible—it is your only chance."

"Doctor, I am rejoiced to meet you in this hour of distress, but doubt the wisdom of your counsel. I am within seventy miles of Virginia [City]. Just over these rocks, a few miles away, I shall find friends. My shoes are nearly worn out, my clothes are in tatters, and my strength is almost overcome. As a last trial, it seems to me I can but attempt to scale this mountain or perish in the effort, if God so wills."

"Don't think of it. Your power of endurance will carry you through. I will accompany you. Put your trust in heaven. Help yourself and God will help you."

Overcome by these and other persuasions, and delighted with the idea of having a traveling companion, I plodded my way over the route I had come, intending at a certain point to change it so as to strike the river at the foot of the lake.

At daybreak I was on the trail down the river. The thought I had adopted from the first— "I will not perish in this wilderness"—often revived my sinking spirits. Once, while struggling through a field of tangled trunks I found myself seriously considering whether it was not preferable to die there than renew the effort to proceed. I felt that all attempt to escape was but a bitter prolongation of the agony of dissolution. A seeming whisper in the air—"While there is life, there is hope; take courage"—broke the delusion, and I clambered on.

I lost all sense of time. Days and nights came and went, numbered only by the growing consciousness that I was gradually starving. I felt no hunger, did not eat to appease appetite, but to renew strength. I experienced but little pain. The gaping sores on my feet, the severe burn on my hip, the festering crevices at the joints of my fingers, all terrible in appearance, had ceased to give me the least concern. The roots which supplied my food had suspended the digestive power of the stomach, and their fibers were packed in it in a matted, compact mass.

Not so with my hours of slumber. They were visited by the most luxurious dreams. I would apparently visit the most gorgeously decorated restaurants of New York and Washington; sit down to immense tables spread with the most appetizing foods; partake of the richest oyster stews and plumpest pies . . .

As night drew on I selected a camping place, gathered wood into a heap, and felt for my lens to procure fire. It was gone. The floodgates of misery seemed now to be opened, and it rushed in living tide upon my soul. With the rapidity of lightning, I ran over every event of my life. Thoughts doubled and trebled upon me, until I saw, as if in vision, the entire past of my existence. It was all before me, as if painted with a sunbeam, and all seemingly faded like the phantoms of a vivid dream.

As calmness returned, reason resumed her empire. Fortunately, the weather was comfortable. I summoned all the powers of my memory, thought over every foot of the day's travel, and concluded that the glass must have become detached from my belt while sleeping. Five long miles over the hills must be retraced to regain it. There was no alternative, and before daylight I had staggered over half the distance. I found the lens on the spot where I had slept. No incident of my journey brought with it more of joy and relief.

A solemn conviction that death was near overwhelmed me with terror. Amid all this tumult of the mind, I felt that I had done all that man could do. I knew that in two or three days more I could effect my deliverance. I derived no little satisfaction from the thought that, as I was now in the broad trail, my remains would be found, and my friends relieved of doubt as to my fate.

Once only the thought flashed across my mind that I should be saved, and I seemed to hear a whispered command to "Struggle on." Groping along the side of a hill, I became suddenly sensible of a sharp reflection, as of burnished steel. Looking up, through half-closed eyes, two rough but kindly faces met my gaze.

"Are you Mr. Everts?"

"Yes. All that is left of him."

"We have come for you."

'Who sent you?"

"Judge Lawrence and other friends."

"God bless him, and them, and you! I am saved!" With these words I fell forward into the arms of my preservers, in a state of unconsciousness. I was saved. On the very brink of the river which divides the known from the unknown, strong arms snatched me from the final plunge, and kind ministrations wooed me back to life.

Baronet and Prichette, my two preservers, soon restored me to consciousness and made a camp upon the spot. One went to Fort Ellis, a distance of seventy miles, to return with remedies to restore digestion and an ambulance to convey me to that post. The other sat by my side, and with all the care, sympathy, and solicitude of a brother, he ministered to my frequent necessities.

In two days I was sufficiently recovered in strength to be moved twenty miles down the trail to the cabin of some miners who were prospecting in that vicinity. From these men I received every possible attention which their humane and generous natures could devise. A good bed was provided, game was killed to make broth, and the best stores of their larder placed at my command. For four days, at a time when every day's labor was invaluable in their pursuit, they abandoned their work to aid in my restoration. Owing to the protracted inaction of the system, and the long period which must transpire before Prichette's return with remedies, my friends had serious doubts of my recovery.

The night after my arrival at the cabin, while suffering the most excruciating agony, and thinking that I had only been saved to die among friends, a loud knock was heard at the cabin door. An old man in mountain costume entered—a hunter, whose life was spent among the mountains. He was on his way to find a brother. He listened to the story of my sufferings, and tears rapidly coursed each other down his rough, weather-beaten face. But when he was told of my present necessity, brightening in a moment, he exclaimed:

"Why, Lord bless you, if that is all, I have the very remedy you need. In two hours' time all shall be well with you."

He left the cabin, returning in a moment with a sack filled with the fat of a bear that he had killed a few hours before. From this he rendered out a pint measure of oil. I drank the whole of it. It proved to be the needed remedy, and the next day, freed from pain, with appetite and digestion reestablished, I felt that only good food and plenty of it were necessary for an early recovery.

In a day or two I took leave of my kind friends, with a feeling of regret at parting, and of gratitude for their kindness as enduring as life. Meeting the carriage along the way, I proceeded to Bozeman, where I remained among old friends, who gave me every attention until my health was sufficiently restored to allow me to return to my home at Helena. ✦

About This Story

Separated from his party without any supplies. Burned by thermal features. Frostbitten from the night air. Weak from starvation. Truman Everts barely survived his visit to Yellowstone.

His tale of surviving thirty-seven days in the wild was the first story from Yellowstone to capture the nation's imagination. There had been expeditions and scientific papers: Everts was, in fact, part of the Washburn-Langford-Doane expedition to explore the region. But no account was quite as gripping as a man facing a mountain lion in the wilderness. Before Everts' story was published in *Scribner's Magazine*, Yellowstone was a growing curiosity. Afterwards, Yellowstone was a national phenomenon.

For a man who found a way to be hurt by all aspects of the landscape, Everts is remembered fondly in Yellowstone, and both Mount Everts and Evert's Thistle, a plant he famously subsisted on during his misadventure, were named after him.

Origin of the Snake and Yellowstone Rivers

RALPH DIXEY

ong ago there was no river in this part of the country. No Snake River ran through the land. During that time a man came up from the south. No one knows what kind of person he was, except that among his people he was always nosing around, always sticking his nose into everything.

He came through this valley, traveled north past Teton, and then went up on a mountain in what is now called the Yellowstone country. He looked around there and soon found an old lady's camp. She had a big basket of fish in water—all kinds of fish—and the man was hungry. So he said to her, "I am hungry. Will you boil some fish for me?"

"Yes, I will cook some for you," the old lady answered. "But don't bother my fish," she warned, as she saw him looking into the basket.

But he did not obey her. While she was busy cooking, he kept nosing around, kept monkeying around. At last he stepped on the edge of the basket and spilled the fish. The water spread all over.

The man ran fast, ahead of the water, and tried to stop it. He piled some rocks up high, in order to hold the waters back. But the water broke his dam and rushed over the rocks. That's where Upper Yellowstone Falls are now. The man ran ahead of the water again, and again he tried to stop it. Four or five miles below Yellowstone Falls he built another pile of rocks. But that didn't hold the water back either. The rush of water broke that dam, too. That's where the Lower Yellowstone Falls are today. The water kept on rushing and formed the Yellowstone River.

Then the man ran to the opposite side of the fish basket, to the other side of the water emptying from it. He built another dam down the valley where Idaho

Falls are now. By the time he got there, the flood had become bigger and swifter. And so, though the man built a big dam, the water broke it and rushed on down the valley.

Again he ran, overtook the water, and built another dam. "Here's where I'm going to stop it," he said to himself. But the water had become bigger and bigger, swifter and swifter. So it broke that dam and left the American Falls where they are today.

The man rushed ahead and built two piles of rocks in the form of a half-circle, one pole where Shoshone Falls are now and one where Twin Falls are now. "I'll really stop the water this time," he said to himself. But the water filled the dam, broke it, and rushed over the rocks in giant waterfalls.

The man ran ahead, down to near where Huntington, Oregon, is today. There the valley narrows into a canyon. "Here's where I'll stop the water," he said, "here between these high hills."

So he built a dam and walked along on top of it, singing and whistling. He was sure he had stopped the water this time. He watched it coming toward him, sure that he would soon see it stop. It filled the dam, broke it, and rushed on down the canyon. Hell's Canyon, it's called today.

Just before the dam broke, the man climbed up on top of the canyon wall.

"I give up," he said, as he watched the water rush through the gorge. "I won't build any more dams. They don't stop that water."

After the river left Hell's Canyon, it became wide again and very swift. The water went on down to Big River and then on down to the ocean, taking with it the big fish that had spilled out of the old lady's basket. That's why we have only small fish up here. Salmon and sturgeon were carried on down to the ocean, and they have never been able to get back up here because of the waterfalls. Salmon used to come up as far as Twin Falls, a long time ago, but they don't come now.

The big fish basket that the man tipped over is Yellowstone Lake. The water that he spilled ran off in two directions. Some of it made the Snake River, as I have told you, and finally reached the Columbia and the Pacific. Some of it ran the other way and made the Yellowstone River and then reached the Missouri River.

Who was the old lady with the basket of water and fish? She was Mother Earth. Who was the man who wanted to see everything, who was always sticking his nose into everything? He was *Ezeppa*, or Coyote. ✦

About This Story

Although there are twenty-six native tribes associated with Yellowstone today, their stories are absent from the records of European explorers. William Clark, of the Lewis & Clark Expedition, surmised that natives were afraid of the geysers—an assumption now widely believed to be absurdly false. More likely is that the natives were intentionally not telling the Europeans about their sacred lands.

The origins of the Yellowstone River is one of the only verified and authentic native stories of the region. This version was told by a Northern Shoshone man named Ralph Dixey, and collected in 1953 by folklorist Ella E. Clark. Other than this story, there is little reliable information or documentation on legends, myths, or other native folklore about Yellowstone. Without Dixey and Clark, we would not know the role that mischievous Coyote played in creating the waterfalls and lakes of Yellowstone.

Editor's Study: I & II

CHARLES DUDLEY WARNER

I.

A lady said that the central portion of the Rocky Mountain region—that is, the Yellowstone Park—is the safety-valve of the United States. There are the vent-holes of its internal fires and explosive energies, and but for the relief they afford, the whole country might be shaken with earthquakes and be blown up in fragments. There is the smoking and vomiting chimney of the continent. There issue the stream, the hot water in fountains and rivers, the explosive gases, the dissolved and triturated minerals and earths, generated in the incandescent bowels of the earth. I heard a soldier say that if the Old Faithful geyser did not go off every sixty-five minutes, he should be alarmed, and should fear to stay in that neighborhood, for no one could tell where this suppressed force might not break out. The mountains look pretty solid around there, though some of them—like the Roaring Mountain, which is so full of steam-vents that it looks like a hill on fire—do not seem promising places to plant vineyards (if grapes would grow 7,500 feet above the sea); the great basins of Hell, the Devil, and other unpleasant names, upon which the steam whirls in clouds, driving over the red-hot ponds and boiling pot-holes, have usually a thin crust, upon which people walk with some courage; but there arises a general want of confidence in the stability of the whole region. It is not encouraging to feel the crust made hot under your feet, and to have to be careful not to step into holes of boiling water, and fissures of unknown depth which vomit steam, fat-frying kettles, boiling pots of paint and mud, and to have to run away from a caldron which suddenly sends into the air a great column of hot water.

All the world knows, from the pens of a thousand descriptive writers and from the photographs, the details of these marvels, so that I need not enter upon them. But I suppose their effect is different upon different persons. How beautiful many of the "formations" are that have been slowly built up by the overflow of these limpid waters which carry so many salts in solution! What a sense of power there is in the spouting geysers! How exquisite in iridescent colors are some of the burning lakes! How lovely the pools of deep emerald, of sapphire! And the graceful steam floating about over this burning world! But it is hot, and it has a sickening smell, like steam from a dirty laundry. I learned to call it the Park smell, so constant it is in the hell-fire regions. It is exciting to watch for the spouting of the geysers, and the recurrence of other intermitting phenomena; but many disagreeable things do not intermit. The pools and pots are always boiling, streams of hot water never stop, and there are steam-vents that roar as constantly as blast-furnaces. One I recall which sends out laterally as from a funnel, with an awful roar, a great volume of super-heated steam, night and day, year after year, in extravagant rage and prodigality. Steam enough is wasted here to run all the Western railways. Where does it come from? This one never takes a day or an hour off, like many of the uneasy friers and spouters in the basin below it. These displays, however, are wholesome in comparison with what is called the mud-geyser, which is, I suppose, the most disgusting object in nature. This horrible thing is not in any of the geyser basins, but has a place to itself on the road between the Lake and the Yellowstone Cañon. On the side of a hill, at the bottom of a deep sloping pit, is a sort of cave, like the lair of a wild beast, which perpetually vomits a compound of mud, putty, nastiness. Over the mouth seems to be a concave rock, which prevents the creature from spouting his filth straight up like a geyser. Against this obstacle, with a thud, every moment the vile fluid is flung, as if the beast were in a rage, and growling because he could not get out, and then through the orifice the mud is flung in spiteful spits and gushes of nastiness. And the most disgusting part of it is that this awful mixture cannot get out, and the creature has to swallow it again, and is perpetually sick to nausea. It is the most fascinatingly loathsome thing in the world. I recalled the dragon and his cave in Wagner's *Siegfried*. There, the reader remembers, is a dark cave, out of which issue volumes of steam and an animal noise. Presently a dragon protrudes his horrid scaly head and fore paws, and from his jaws come flame and steam. The contrivance seems to have been suggested by this mud-geyser. In this geyser I have no doubt there is a dragon, but he can never get his head out. You can only hear him rage, and you can see the nastiness he vomits out.

II.

Bewildering as all this spectacle is to one's idea of a normal and orderly world, I was more impressed by what I could not see than by these strange surface phenomena. It is what is underneath this thin crust, it is the state of things underground, that appeals to the imagination. Where does all this inexhaustible supply of steam and limpid hot water and dissolved salts and paint and liquid mud come from? The crust is hot and trembling. We must be walking, amid boiling pots and pits, over a terrible furnace. How far below is this furnace? Are these hot substances thrown up from the centre, or is the earth, only a little distance under us, all molten and fluid and a raging hell? Why does it not burst up everywhere and blow this whole mountain region sky-high? Here and there in this vast territory one sees frightful fields and ravines of shapeless, contorted rocks, as if in those places the interior had exploded, and created and left ruin. And yet there is a process of creation in sight, going on daily and yearly, the slow formation of terraces and mounds and well-curbs, all exquisitely sculptured, now like lace-work, now like the chiselling of a sculptor. Are these lovely things created only to be destroyed in a great upheaval of the internal forces? Will the "formations" at the Mammoth Hot Springs and in the geyser basins some day, any day, go up in a vast explosion, and be destroyed and buried in mud, as were recently the similar terraces and formations in New Zealand? What insurance company would take a risk on these things?

In the presence of this immense energy and fiery agitation we seem to be witnesses of the processes of creation, of the primitive evolutionary forces that are making the planet. Of course I know that the earth is not yet created. The lower Mississippi region is now being made before our eyes, as the Nile delta is. What I should like to know is whether the Yellowstone region is now in process of creation, whether it is to be within certain calculable periods greatly changed in form, or whether we are witnessing now the expiring energies of a world gradually cooling down into rigidity and death. The intermittent geysers would seem to intimate that the internal forces are weakening. The great Excelsior geyser, which was so active in 1889, which shook the whole region when it went off, and deluged the neighborhood with an immense flow of hot water, and liberated itself by tearing open an orifice of half an acre in area, is a horrible pit of boiling water and steam, and its opening is now so large that it will probably not be able to send up a column of water again. Still there is no doubt energy here enough to outlast our time, and perhaps our nation, and there can be little doubt that this region acts as a safety-valve of the continent, which would be shaken with earthquakes if these vents were stopped up. ✦

About This Story

Yellowstone is a wonderland. It's a profound place, deep and inspiring. But can we be real? It also smells bad. Humorist Charles Dudley Warner drops the niceties to speak frankly about the unpleasant aspects of the park.

In an early advertisement, Alice (of *Alice in Wonderland*) writes a letter to her cousin Edith, "You never saw, nor could you ever imagine, such strange sights as greet us here at every turn." We couldn't help but laugh as Warner describes it more frankly as "vile" and "disgusting." Such are the side effects of being atop an active supervolcano, one that is responsible for up to three thousand (mostly) small earthquakes annually, and over half of the world's geysers.

Wolf

LUCY JANE BLEDSOE

I wasn't exactly happy with Jim wanting to change his name to Anatoly, but I tried to roll with it. Change is good in a relationship, right? That was the whole reason we went to Yellowstone in the first place, to zest up our marriage, have a little fun, do something new.

I didn't think we needed an overhaul, though. Nor did I think the change needed to bleed outside our marriage. But after the first trip to the park, he started asking our neighbors to call him Anatoly. It was embarrassing.

"Been reading our Dostoyevsky, have we?" said our next-door neighbor Clarence, pleased with himself for dredging up a literary reference.

The other next-door neighbor, Walter, narrowed his eyes, assessed, and then shrugged—neither agreeing nor disagreeing, pretty much just dismissing. I imagined both of them telling their wives, Cathy and Shawna, and having a good laugh on our behalf. Little did I know back then that I needn't have worried about the neighbors; we'd soon be selling the house.

Still, in the beginning, I tried to find the humor myself. My complaints for the 30-plus years we'd been together clustered around sameness, a hazy boredom that occasionally drifted through our otherwise happy marriage. So a new name? Why not? It didn't occur to me that it might signify an entire identity change.

Anatoly means east or sunrise. Fitting, I suppose. But how did he know that? Had he been researching wild names before we even visited the park and met the wolf watchers? I heard him tell them his name was Anatoly that very first morning, but I thought I'd misheard. He'd removed his mitten and thrust out his hand, and the reluctant recipient of his greeting had ignored the hand but nodded when Jim said, "Anatoly." I was barely awake and figured he'd made some obscure joke the other man didn't get. I got back in the car and unscrewed the thermos lid, poured myself some coffee.

The ranger had told us that the wolves were most active at dawn and dusk, and that the best way to view them was to look for the cluster of people beside the road with viewing scopes. It was the dead of January, but sure enough that morning as we drove out the northern park road and entered the Lamar Valley, we found seven people in one of the pullouts, standing with alert expectation in front of fat cylinders on long legs.

Clouds obscured the stars. The sky was black and the snow, a deep lavender. We parked our Ford Fiesta next to the fleet of SUVs, and that's when Jim introduced himself as Anatoly. Forgive me for repeating that moment; it's the part of this life shift I can't explain. The name must have to come to him in the way dreams lay out whole stories we don't even know exist in our unconscious. A wild name, Anatoly, parked in the recesses of Jim's psyche, perhaps for years, waiting for the right mix of circumstances to surface. Or maybe the sight of that black sky and lavender snow, the promise of those long-legged scopes, birthed the name right then and there.

For a few minutes I watched my husband from the car. He asked questions and received brief answers from some of the wolf watchers. Others ignored him. A couple pointedly never even looked at him. I saw him tamp down his eagerness, realize that there was a culture here that he best observe rather than blunder.

This was my first moment of capitulation, although I certainly didn't recognize it as such at the time. Viewing my husband through the windshield, as if it were a lens that allowed me to see him objectively, I saw a man in longing. For what, I couldn't have said, but my annoyance at his enthusiasm for a predawn adventure dissolved. He was thrilled to be there, lured by the mystery of wolves, hoping to experience something new. I couldn't fault him on that. Whatever malaise had settled over our life together, Jim himself had always had a childlike curiosity that I loved. I opened the door and stepped back into the bitter cold air.

The ridge to the east darkened, and the sky directly above it lightened. The mustard yellow burgeoned into a tangerine orange, and then came the first rays of the sun, sheer daggers of light.

A wolf howled.

The wolf watchers aligned themselves with their scopes and began scanning. Jim opened his mouth to ask a question, and I put my mitten against his lips and shook my head. He nodded his thanks, knew that I was right about silence now. The wolf howled again.

Jim looked over his shoulder, as if the beast was about to pounce on him, and then did a quick 360-degree search. I thought he was startled, maybe frightened, but then I realized that the look on his face was deep calm, intense concentration. That howling wolf spoke to his heart more directly than the cries of our babies had.

That night, while Jim was in the shower, I called Barbara from our room at the Mammoth Hot Springs Hotel and told her, "Your father has fallen in love with a female alpha wolf."

"Meaning?" I could hear the background clanking of dinner pots.

"There's this culture of people who go into the park every single day, and they stay all day, looking for the wolf packs."

"Why?"

"I don't know."

"And this has what to do with Dad?"

"I think he does know."

"Call Mark. Have him talk to Dad."

"Mark," I said a few moments later, "I think your dad is considering joining a wolf pack."

Mark laughed. "Sounds about right."

"It does? How so?"

"He has that wandering in him."

This almost offended me. "He's never wandered from us."

"No. But essentially he's a nomad."

Separate. Quiet. Restless. Yes, the word fit, but I didn't like it.

"That's crazy," I said. "What are you talking about?"

"It just always seemed like he needed a passion." Mark hesitated, not wanting to hurt my feelings. "He's always been a little bit sad. Not a lot. But a little bit."

"And a wolf pack is going to make him not sad?"

"It might."

Clearly there would be no advantage to putting Mark on the phone with his father. Nor could I make myself tell him that I thought Jim had introduced himself to the wolf watchers as Anatoly.

"Hey, it's not another woman," Mark laughed. "Not a human one, anyway."

"That's very comforting."

"What did Barbara say?"

"She said to call you."

Two hours after sunrise that first morning, the Lamar Canyon pack was spotted. "Got 'em," said one of the three gray-bearded observers. Later I'd know them as Joe, Gregory, and Zack, but it wasn't until the next trip that I could tell them apart. He spoke quietly, but with a load of triumph.

"Where?" everyone asked in unison, and the man identified a ridge in the distance, began describing clusters of trees, shapes of long shadows on the snow, and snags that could not be seen with the naked eye.

Jim literally squirmed with the desire to see. One of the gray beards motioned him over to his scope. He spoke quietly, explaining that the alpha female was to the far left, out in front, and that four other pack members were running along behind her.

"Let me adjust the scope," he said. "They've probably run out of view already."

I saw the others slide their scope handles to the right, following the running wolves. Jim looked again after the adjustment and almost cried out in his joy. He held back the cry, though, and won points, I'm sure, with the viewing pack.

"Did you see?" the gray beard asked, and Jim nodded.

What I saw was my husband's relationship to those wolves. It was visceral, visual and audible both, as if I could see and hear his heart bursting out of his chest and whizzing out to that pack of freely running canines.

"She . . . " he said to me later in the car. "She . . . " So moved he couldn't finish his sentence, but I knew he was talking about the alpha female, her silvery coat and sprightly legs, her clarity of purpose.

The next morning, we returned to the Lamar Valley well before sunrise, and this time the pack was in the valley itself, playing and resting, only a few hundred yards away. The wolf watchers saw my husband's serious caring, and they began to feed him tidbits of information about this particular pack and especially about the alpha female. Eventually the pack headed at a trot over the ridge to the west, and in under 10 seconds, the watchers had loaded their scopes into the backs of their vehicles and taken off down the road. Jim and I looked at each other in dismay, confused for a moment, but he caught right on.

"They're going to the next pullout where they hope to see the pack come over the ridge toward them." He was at the wheel of the Ford Fiesta before I'd even lowered my binoculars. I swear he might have driven off without me if I hadn't hopped to, so eager he was to see the pack crest the ridge with the rest of the watchers.

Thankfully our short holiday ended. We were both expected back at work on Monday. I chose to think of the whole experience as a positive infusion of joy and adventure, especially for Jim. He told everyone about the wolves. He also told everyone to please call him Anatoly.

I snapped after about two weeks of this. "Tell me," I begged, "what's wrong with the name Jim? It's been good enough for 52 years."

My question brought on what I soon learned to call The Look. His gaze slid past me, way past me, over the buildings of town, beyond the fields of the regional park, far beyond. Is it possible to look farther away than a horizon? Jim did. Anatoly did.

We returned to Yellowstone a month later. In the meantime, he read every book there was to read and followed the 10 park packs—and the two loners—on the websites of the wolf watchers. He knew how to identify the alpha males and females, the names and ranges of the packs. The Mollies, he told me, lived just north of the lake, while the Canyon, Blacktail, and Agate packs had territories to the west of the Lamar Canyon Pack.

"Eleven packs," I told him as we approached the park. He glanced at me, knowing I was including the odd group of people who organized their entire lives around viewing the wolves in Yellowstone, but he was immune to criticism on this front. He merely nodded at my comment. It was like he was a lone wolf on the periphery, looking for a way to be admitted to the pack. Knowledge was always valuable, and he'd armed himself with lots. So was acquiescent behavior, and he greeted the group quietly our first morning of this second trip, nodding like they did, setting up his scope, scanning the ridgetops with his binoculars. He pretended he'd already been accepted.

I'm surprised he brought me along. Couldn't I be considered a liability? Sure, one astute male who was apparently willing to buy into every single rule had a chance, but I was a dubious female, suspicious, circling on the outside, quite ready to attack from a psychological point of view. I granted these people what I thought was a generous assessment: They were passionate. But where is the line between passion and obsession?

Take Michelle, maybe 45 years old, evidently unemployed, she rose before the sun each and every morning and drove into the park to view wolves. At least Louise and Gregory were retired, or so I assumed by their ages, and they shared the fixation with one another. Ashley and Neil, another couple, were not old enough to be retired, nor did they exhibit a shared delight in the wolf pursuit. In fact, their quiet and infrequent, but forceful nonetheless, banter revealed a deep competitiveness.

"Got her," Neil said on our first morning back in the park.

"Oh, you mean 54?" Ashley responded with strained cheeriness. "I've been watching her for five minutes."

After an irritated pause, Neil said, "That would be impossible, dear. She came over the ridge 17 seconds ago."

"Hon?" Syrupy. "You're talking about 31. He"—the pronoun emphasis pointing out that Neil had gotten even the sex of the animal wrong—"is right there next to the closest tree. You're right about that."

"Oh, 31?" Neil retorted. "He's been there since before sunrise. I recognized his voice, which made it quite clear that he was somewhere in that stand of alders."

Ashley swung her scope 45 degrees to the right, as if she'd suddenly become aware of a whole new wolf situation and Neil, who'd pulled back from his scope for the argument, couldn't resist pushing his eye back against the eyepiece and swinging his that way, too. I bet there was nothing there at all. Ashley was just messing with Neil.

The entire group usually stayed all day, until the last possible chance of a sighting at dusk. "See you in the morning!" they'd call out quietly at the end of the day, packing up their scopes. On our last night in the park that second trip, Jim and I overheard them making arrangements to have dinner together. Michelle was cooking spaghetti for everyone at her place just outside Silver Gate. Jim was hurt that we hadn't been invited.

"Why would we be?" I asked him, appalled at his feeling of belonging. "We don't know these people. We have lives 200 miles away, a house, grown children, and grandchildren. We have jobs."

After dinner in our hotel, while Jim interrogated a wildlife tour guide he'd found in the lobby, I sat on a nearby couch and called Barbara. I felt as if I shouldn't let him out of my sight, though I couldn't name what it was I feared.

"Mom, it's late. I'm trying to get the kids to bed."

"I know," I whispered, feeling as if I were betraying Jim by telling on him to our children.

"We're back in the park."

"You mean Yellowstone?"

"Yes."

Barbara paused, and I was gratified that she was finally getting the situation. "So that Dad can look for wolves again?"

"Yes."

In her silence I heard her decide that she couldn't do anything about my problem. "Girls," she called to her daughters. "You want to say hi to Grandma?"

After she put them each on an extension, I greeted my two granddaughters, 3 and 5 years old, by telling them, "Your grandpa wants to become a wolf."

The older one, Bella, giggled, but Heidi said nothing. I may have scared her. Bella said, "Grandma, that's not possible. That only happens in fairytales."

"True," I forced myself to admit.

There was no call for frightening my grandchildren. Nor was it fair to hope for support from five- and three-year-olds. But children can sometimes believe the unbelievable, and I needed someone to witness this change in my husband. Bella snickered again, and Heidi started to ask a question, but Barbara took the phones away from them and announced bedtime. I heard shrieking, and Barbara hung up without saying goodbye. She often assumed rudeness was okay in the wake of parenting, and that I'd understand having had two children myself, but I could have used a "goodbye" and "I love you."

Two weeks later, we were back in Yellowstone, and this time Anatoly had me drop him off in Lamar Valley. We both doubted very much that the National Park Service condoned camping in the backcountry, at least not here in the most common wolf territory, but there was no talking him out of it. I tried the tactic of telling him that if Joe, Gregory, Zack, Michelle, Ashley, Louise, or Neil found out, he'd be shunned. Not disturbing the wolves in their habitat was the supreme rule.

Never mind the fact that he'd never camped a day in his life. Here we were, though, in the Lamar Valley, in the pitch black of extreme early morning, so he could get out of sight before the wolf watchers arrived. He'd outfitted himself with a backpack, tent, stove, and snowshoes. I insisted on no meat products in his pack, which he agreed was a good idea, but nothing else I suggested held any weight.

I love my husband and I feared for his life, I truly did, but after 30 years of marriage you do learn that you can't stop anyone from doing something they want to do. You really can't. And in the case of my husband sleeping with the wolves, "want" wasn't an even close approximation to the verb needed to describe what Anatoly was after.

The problem was getting him out, and hopefully back, without anyone seeing him. Even though he was setting out well before the wolf watchers arrival, I dropped him far from any of the pullouts, and then he had to hoof it fast, headlamp strapped to his forehead, to get out of sight of the road. How he'd get back to the road the next day, without being spotted, I didn't know. Or even care. By this time I thought his arrest might be the best outcome.

I lay in bed that night, back in the Mammoth Hot Springs Hotel, reading a book. I'd already gone to the ranger talk and eaten a multicourse dinner, to pass the time, but there was no television reception out there, so I was left with a book and my thoughts. I'll spare you the gratuitous details of those. I did sleep for a couple of hours.

The next day I sat in the Ford Fiesta, the engine running so that I could have heat, and scanned the landscape with my binoculars. Earlier, as I scraped the ice off the windows of the car in the dark, I felt like a fool. Why I had allowed this, I didn't know. I should have insisted on a counselor. I could have refused to be an accomplice. He wouldn't have been able to get anyone else to help him. I could have put a stop to the whole enterprise.

Instead I had dropped the man off in the soul of February, temperatures barely hovering over zero degrees, in wolf country. My own husband. Seriously, I was the one who should have made an appointment with a counselor.

"You're enabling," Barbara had told me a few days earlier.

Mark only laughed, angering me with his blithe reaction. Men supporting men's harebrained schemes.

What had I done? Introducing my husband as Anatoly was an embarrassment. But explaining that he'd lost his life because I left him off in wolf country in the middle of a winter night was probably criminal.

I saw a dot on the snowy ridge. A moving dot. Just one, with two legs. I trained my binoculars on the animal and whispered, "Got 'im."

As my husband loped toward me, I checked his gait for a limp. None. As he drew even closer, I looked for blood or pain on his face. Again, none.

I'd wanted him to live, of course, but I realized then that I'd also hoped for pain, for a terrifying experience that would cure him of this newfound love of the wild. Hope and expectation are two different things, though, and seeing that he was fine, just fine, I shifted into the latter. I knew what I would see when he reached the car. A hard, wolfish stare. Maybe a growl. Claims of spiritual visitations. I half-expected him to have found a downed animal and be hauling the pelt, maybe wearing it draped across his shoulders. We'd gone past the chance of a counselor helping us. We'd need an intervention.

Jim pulled the door of the passenger seat open and stuck in his head. "Open the trunk?" I heard him dump his sodden backpack on top of the extra jackets and boots, followed by a clacking of snowshoes, and then he was back at the passenger door, opening it, and dropping into the seat. Would he howl at me?

For the first time I wished for the company of Joe, Gregory, Zack, Michelle, Ashley, Louise, and Neil. Unfortunately, the wolf watchers were in a different part of the park that day, but if they'd been there, they surely would have reported my husband to the Park Service and every other wildlife protection agency. They would never again allow him to set up his scope alongside theirs. He would be a pariah, this man who would disturb the wolves, who believed that he alone could beat his own DNA, join, even for a night, a different species. But they weren't there, so I was left on my own to accept my husband's experience.

After settling into the seat, he turned and looked at me. His eyes were soft. Actually, his entire body was soft, almost slumped, loose and happy, like after the best sex. I looked for the part of him that yearned back toward the ridge, but it wasn't there. He was looking at me.

"Sweetie," he said. "Thank you."

"Thank you?"

"I mean, wow. That was unbelievably scary. And beautiful. And awesome. And here you are, to pick me up. Thank you."

"Did you see them?"

He shook his head. "No. But I heard them. A lot. And just being there. With them, within their range, in their habitat. I know they smelled me, knew I was there."

"I suppose so."

"They did."

I nodded and wondered if I could start driving now.

"I don't think any of the others saw me."

The others. I wished he meant that word, others, as in as opposed to him, but I knew he didn't. He meant others as in others in his own group. His pack.

"They wouldn't approve, Jim. They'd be very angry."

"I know. It was wrong of me. It was just something I had to do. And I knew I had to do it soon, and fast, before I realized the full wrongness of it. Do you know what I mean?"

Understanding came to me in a flash, maybe in the same way the name Anatoly came to Jim, something I'd known all along, a willingness that just needed the right set of conditions to emerge. His gray eyes were still looking at me, directly, and they were full of love. For me, yes, but I saw that the love also encompassed much more: the mountains and wolves, himself. It made me think how we were just two people making a life in a vast world that we barely glimpsed. I thought of how our marriage had sometimes felt like a tar pit: jobs, illnesses, housework, and difficult communication sucking us ever deeper into a thick, gooey place. But all along, beyond the pit, was this open wildness infused with love.

"You do know what I mean, don't you?" he said.

I did.

He took my hand. "Please."

"Okay," I said.

We bought the four-wheel drive so we could manage icy roads. On our fourth trip, we got invited to dinner with the others. The look on my husband's face was more biological satisfaction than happiness; it was as if they'd thrown a chunk of raw elk at his feet. But the thing was, these people turned out to be more regular than I'd expected. Everyone shared stories over the beers and spaghetti, but not just wolf stories. They had children and grandchildren. Some had traveled all over the world. Most had left jobs that had pinned them to lives that had become untenable. Each of them now pursued wolves full-time, pretty much every day, winter, spring, summer, and fall.

At the end of the evening they said, "See you in the morning."

Within the year, we took early retirements and bought a house just outside the park. Our son Mark finally became concerned. I supposed he was worried about having to support us in our dotage. He should have thought of that at the beginning, when there might have been a chance of talking his father out of the new lifestyle. Barbara surprised me by cheering us on. She and Jason brought the kids out right away, and while they didn't have the patience for wolves, they loved seeing the bison and elk and coyotes.

I've never let myself forget how crazy it looks from the outside. And I'll never be as devoted as Jim. Some days I stay home. In fact, I found a part-time job in Gardiner, to give us a bit of cash to supplement our retirement income.

Jim dropped the Russian name. That was just a portal, he said. He couldn't enter the wild as an aging man from suburbia. He had needed to slip out of the jumpsuit of his life, but he was afraid to stand naked. Anatoly was a costume, he said, one that conjured wailing winds and cold snow, a distraction that would allow his transformation.

"So now you're naked?" our son asked, smirking, no longer male bonding.

"Yes," Jim answered. "You don't know until you've heard them howl." ✦

About This Story

Every morning, amid the beautiful rolling hills of the Lamar Valley in the eastern end of the park, a strange pack of creatures gather with coffee in one hand, scopes and tripods in the other. These are the wolf watchers, the men and women who have devoted their lives to observing the wild wolves that were reintroduced to Yellowstone National Park in 1995.

Bledsoe's story explores the curious culture of the wolf watchers, a group as unique as the wolves they love, with observable social cues and pack behavior. But *Wolf* also illustrates the powerful pull of being chosen by nature. It's one that we can relate to. That inexplicable draw to the wilderness, one that you can't quite explain, but know that you have to fulfill.

Acknowledgments

This book would not have been realized without the support, encouragement, and enthusiasm of our wonderful community of friends, family, mentors, and the individuals across the country who took the time to sit down with us over coffee or in any of the six incredible national parks we visited. We'd like to take a moment to thank those individuals for their contributions to our book.

First, to our friends and family who continually encourage and support our creative endeavors without question.

To Melissa McFeeters, whose patience and eye for detail is the reason the book is so beautifully and meticulously designed. To Kerry Gilbert, Stuart Romanek, and Theresa Decker who helped us take *Campfire Stories* beyond the book to the physical and digital realms.

To Dr. Anna Beresin who provided invaluable insights in preparation for this "fishing expedition" and pushed us to share our personal narrative. To Sarah Low, for her mentorship and general unmatched spirit and enthusiasm.

To Christine Zapata who returned from a fearless thru-hike of the Appalachian Trail and cared for our home and our sweet Tuuli, Samson, and Pencil while we were on the road. To Ruth Scott Blackson for being our soul neighbor and secret keeper, for checking in weekly and helping us stay calm and excited about the news of our little one.

To the fine folks at The Head and Hand Press who supported us from the very beginning, before we had anything other than an idea—especially Linda Gallant Moore and Connor Mannion for their early editing help. To James Edward Mills who supported our project from the very start, and who continues to promote the book and support us.

To Brendan O'Keefe and Jarly Bobadilla at The Howling Woods in Southwest Harbor, Maine, and Anna Davis, David Levinson, Tess Faller, and Moses at Beech Hill Farm who kindly sheltered us in barns, cabins, and longhouses during our travels around Mount Desert Island. To Geo Neptune and Tim Garrity who went above and beyond to show and teach us the history of your beautiful island on the sea. To the staff at Jesup Memorial Library in Bar Harbor, Maine, and

Candy Emlen at the Southwest Harbor Public Library who provided us with invaluable source material for the book and shelter from the elements.

To Ila Hatter and Jerry Coleman for welcoming us into their Smokies mountain home, feeding us and sharing their warmth and wisdom. To Curt Buchholtz of the National Park Foundation for shuttling us around to share your love and extensive knowledge of the Rocky Mountains with us. To Kylie and Kathy Chappell who kindly hosted us at the Flying Spur and shared their history and love of Yosemite with us. To our dear friend Laura Wattles who offered us shelter, a shower, a kitchen, a refrigerator, a puppy, air conditioning, and laughs at a time when we really needed it. To Penny Otwell for sharing her art and love of Yosemite with us.

To those who took the time to connect us to the right folks or meet with us before and during our travels:

Lillian Dunn, Kevin Burke, Sophie Sarkar, Julie Judkins and Javier Folgar of the Appalachian Trail Conservancy, Ellen Heier of the Every Kid in a Park Initiative, George Neptune, Ralph Stanley, Elmer Beal, Jack Russell, Diver Ed, Bill Carpenter at the College of the Atlantic, Nicole Ouellette, Hope Lewis, Ron and Karen Greenberg, Michele Marks, Brittany Parker and Andrew Simon of the Barn Arts Collective, the Roanoke Chapter of the Friends of the Blue Ridge Parkway, Steve Kemp and Laurel Rematore of the Great Smoky Mountains Association, Brent McDaniel of the Friends of the Smokies, Ranger Grace Dyer, Courtney Lix, Dr. Barbara Duncan at the Museum of the Cherokee Indian, Jeremiah Wolfe, the Smoky Mountain Storytellers Association (Rick Elliott, Jim Eastin, Cuz Headrick, and Janice Brooks-Headrick), Robin Goddard, Beth Sutton of the Great Smoky Mountains Heritage Center, Nancy Wilson of the Rocky Mountain Conservancy, Kurtis Kelly, Carie Essig of the Lula Dorsey Museum at the YMCA of the Rockies, park ranger Kathy Brazelton, park ranger Harry Canon, Dave Lively, park ranger Jamie Mansfield, park ranger Sarah Horton, park ranger Adrienne Fitzgerald, Robert and Mary Cox, Scott Williams, Michael Plyler of the Zion Canyon Field Institute, Lyman Hafen of the Zion Natural History Association, park ranger Benn Pikyavit, Charley Bulletts, park ranger Jamie Richards, park ranger Moses Chun, Adonia Ripple of the Yosemite Conservancy, Reed Schneider of NatureBridge, Michael Wise of the Ansel Adams Gallery, Brenda Ostrom, the folks at Rush Creek

Lodge, Ranger Ben Cunningham- Summerfield, Ken Yager of Yosemite Facelift, park ranger Shelton Johnson, Clark Tonkin, Ken Voorhis and Neil Mathieu of Yellowstone Forever, Linda and Luke Black Elk, park ranger Amy Rether, Lee Whittlesey, Sandra Sallee, Paul Shea, Jim Garry, and Bob Richard.

And finally, this project was made possible by over 350 backers on Kickstarter who believed in our idea and project, and whose support gave us the courage and assurance to pursue this book. Special thanks to the following supporters who pledged $100 or more:

Anthony Guido, Alexis Rosenzweig, Andreas Heldal-Lund, Angela Kim, Bob Hanlon, Christian Gray, Craig Irrgang, Dave Hickethier, Diane Shapiro, Elizabeth Miller, Frederick William VanDuyne IV, Geoff DiMasi, Jenny Kim, Jessica Rosenzweig, Johnny Bates, Jorren Schauwaert, Justin Kunkel, Kevin Lee, Kimberly Carroll-Pincus, Linda Rosenzweig, Mark Kandrysawtz, Mary Ann Young, Matej Hrescak, Molly Ann Monahan, Ok Sook Kim, Patricia Leung, Ruth Scott Blackson, Sadie Tettemer, Sean Shapiro, Robert Shapiro, Sharne Algotsson, Sheldon Shapiro, Sloan Miller, and Todd Bressi.

Sources

The editors have made every effort to locate all of the copyright holders for the excerpts included in this book. In some cases, however, they were unable to locate the appropriate person or entity or confirm the publication date or other relevant details. If anyone has information on any of the poems, stories, or essays included here, please contact the editors at hello@campfirestoriesbook.com.

Abbey, Edward. "Benedictio." In *Earth Apples: The Poetry of Edward Abbey*, edited by David Peterson, 110. New York: St. Martin's Griffin, 1995.

Acadia National Park
Beal, Elmer. "The Burning Tree." Song lyrics provided by the author.

Blanchard, Peter P., III. *We Were an Island: The Maine Life of Art & Nan Kellam*. 22–28. Hanover, NH: ©2010 University Press of New England. Reprinted with permission.

Carpenter, Bill. "Fire." In *Maine Speaks: An Anthology of Maine Literature*. 267–68. Brunswick: Maine Writers and Publishers Alliance, 1989.

Moore, Ruth. "The Ballad of the Night Charley Tended Weir." In *Cold as a Dog and the Wind Northeast: Ballads by Ruth Moore*, 9–20. Camden, ME: Timberhead, Inc., 1986. Reprinted with permission from the estate of Ruth Moore.

Neptune, Geo. "Koluskap naka Pukcinsqehs: of Koluskap and the Witch that loved him." Abbe Museum Core Exhibit. People of the First Light. Bar Harbor, ME.

Nicolar, Joseph. "The Coming of Glooskap." In *Maine Speaks: An Anthology of Maine Literature*, 132–33. Brunswick: Maine Writers and Publishers Alliance, 1989.

Excerpts from Williams, Terry Tempest. "Acadia National Park, Maine." In *The Hour of Land: A Personal Topography of America's National Parks*, 85–93. New York: Sarah Crichton Books, 2016. Reprinted by permission of Farrar, Straus and Giroux.

Great Smoky Mountains National Park
Excerpt(s) from Bryson, Bill. "Chapter 15." In *A Walk in the Woods: Rediscovering America on the Appalachian Trail*, 190–93. New York: Broadway Books, 1997. All rights reserved.

Hembree, James Willis. "Prelude." In *Smoky Mountain Songs*, 15–17. Boston: Christopher Publishing House, 1931.

Littlejohn, Kathi Smith. "The Birds and Animals Stickball Game." In *Living Stories of the Cherokee*, edited by Barbara R. Duncan, 66–68. Chapel Hill: University of North Carolina Press, 1998. Used by permission of the publisher. www.uncpress.unc.edu

Oakley, Wiley. "When a small little chap . . ." In *Roamin': With the Roamin' Man of the Smoky Mountains*, 11–16. Gatlinburg, TN: Oakley Books, 1986.

Owle, Freeman. "The Removed Townhouses." In *Living Stories of the Cherokee*, edited by Barbara R. Duncan, 239–243. Chapel Hill, NC: University of North Carolina Press, 1998. Used by permission of the publisher. www.uncpress.unc.edu

Parris, John. "A Valley of Memories." In *These Storied Mountains*, 135–37. Asheville, NC: Asheville Citizen-Times, 1972. © 1972 Gannett-Community Publishing. All rights reserved.

Pratt, Doug, performer. *That Good Old Mountain Dew*. Doug Pratt, 1968, cassette. Oral History Collection. Anna Porter Public Library. Gatlinburg, TN.

Rocky Mountain National Park

Bird, Isabella. "Letter VII." In *A Lady's Life in the Rocky Mountains*, 83–101. Norman: University of Oklahoma Press, 1960.

Buchholtz, C. W. *Secret Elk Study Revealed*. Unpublished manuscript. Provided by the author.

Campbell, SueEllen. "Yellow-Bellied Marmots." In *A Poetic Inventory of Rocky Mountain National Park*, 68–69. Fort Collins, CO: Wolverine Farm Publishing, 2013.

Hewes, Charles Edwin. "Rocky Mountain National Park Colorado." In *Songs of the Rockies*, 1. Hewes-Kirkwood, CO: The Egerton-Palmer Press, 1922.

Mills, Enos. "Children of My Trail School." In *Adventures of a Nature Guide*, 89–91. Estes Park, CO: Temporal Mechanical Press, 2001.

Moomaw, Jack C. "Other Campfires: Ancient Walls on Trail Ridge." In *Recollections of a Rocky Mountain Ranger*, 119–21. Estes Park, CO: YMCA of the Rockies, 1994.

Robinson, Bill. "The Legend of the Blue Mist." In *The Blue Mist: An Estes Park Legend*, 19–37. Estes Park, CO: YMCA of the Rockies, 1991.

Romig, Edna Davis. "The Mountains Rise." In *These are the Fields*, 20. Philadelphia: Dorrance & Company, 1955.

Zion National Park

Chesher, Greer. "The Language of Zion." In *Zion Canyon: A Storied Land*, 3–9. Tucson: The University of Arizona Press, 2007.

Crawford, J. L. "The Ghosts of Zion." Presented at the 75th Anniversary Celebration of Zion. Springdale, UT: July 31, 1984.

Palmer, William R. comp. "Why the North Star Stands Still." In *Why the North Star Stands Still and Other Indian Legends*, 71–75. Springdale, UT: Zion Natural History Association, 1978.

Williams, Terry Tempest. "The Coyote Clan." In *Red: Passion and Patience in the Desert*, 23–26. New York: Pantheon Books, 2002. Appeared in slightly different form by Peregrine Smith Layton, 1989. Used by permission of Brandt & Hochman Literary Agents, Inc. All rights reserved.

Woodbury, Angus M. "The Great White Throne." In *A Zion Canyon Reader*, 132–39. Salt Lake City: The University of Utah Press, 2014.

Yosemite National Park

Blaney, Carol. "Summit Fever." In *Yosemite Poets: A Gathering of This Place*, edited by Bridget McGinniss Kerr, 30. Tollhouse, CA: Scrub Jay Press, 2010.

Johnson, Shelton. "horse heaven." In *Gloryland*, 225–29. San Francisco, CA: Sierra Club Books, 2009. Reprinted by permission of Counterpoint.

Johnson, Shelton. "lombard gate." In *Gloryland*, 153–56. San Francisco, CA: Sierra Club Books, 2009. Reprinted by permission of Counterpoint.

Muir, John. "Among the Animals of the Yosemite." In *Our National Parks*, 172–78. Boston and New York: Houghton Mifflin, 1901.

Neely, William L. "Notes From My Tuolumne Journal." *Yosemite Nature Notes* XXXIX, no. 3 (March 1960): 41. Courtesy of the Yosemite Park National Archives.

Pena, Frank La, Craig D. Bates, and Steven P. Medley, comps. "The Legend of Tu-tok-a-nu'-la." In *Legends of the Yosemite Miwok*, 37–38. Yosemite National Park, CA: Yosemite Association, 2007. Reproduced by permission of the compilers. A version of this story originally appeared in "Tribes of California," by Stephen Powers, 1976.

Sanford, Gail Jensen. "Spring Afternoon, Merced River Near the Ahwahnee." In *Yosemite Poets*: A Gathering of This Place, edited by Bridget McGinniss Kerr, 32. Tollhouse, CA: Scrub Jay Press, 2010.

Sargent, Shirley. "Tuolumne Tomboy." In *Enchanted Childhoods: Growing Up in Yosemite, 1864–1945*, 91–96. Yosemite: Ponderosa Press, 1993.

Yellowstone National Park

Bledsoe, Lucy Jane. *Wolf*. Reprinted by permission of DeFiore and Company, on behalf of Lucy Jane Bledsoe. Copyright © 2013 by Lucy Jane Bledsoe.

Carpenter, E. M. "Yellowstone." *New Age*, Nov. & Dec 1943. Courtesy National Park Service, Yellowstone National Park.

Dixey, Ralph. "Origin of the Snake and Yellowstone Rivers." In *Indian Legends from the Northern Rockies*, edited by Ella E. Clark, 174–77. Norman: University of Oklahoma Press, 1988. © 1966; permission conveyed through Copyright Clearance Center, Inc.

Everts, Truman. "Thirty-Seven Days of Peril." *Scribner's Monthly*, November 1841, 1–17.

Helmuth, William Tod. "Yellowstone Park and How It Was Named." In *A Yellowstone Reader: The National Park in Folklore, Popular Fiction, and Verse*, edited by Richard L. Saunders, 21–25. Salt Lake City: The University of Utah Press, 2003.

Warner, Charles Dudley. "Editor's Study: I & II." In *Harper's*. January 1897, 320–25. From *Old Yellowstone Days*, edited by Paul Schullery, 160–63. Boulder, CO: Colorado Associated University Press, 1979.

Park Communities

Each national park attracts its own unique ecosystem of people. Here are some of the friends groups, park advocates and allies, and community organizations we discovered that make each of the six national parks we visited vibrant.

Acadia National Park

ABBE MUSEUM

With the mission to inspire new learning about the Wabanaki Nations with every visit, the Abbe Museum offers changing exhibitions and a robust programming schedule for all ages, welcoming 30,000 visitors each year. Wabanaki people are actively engaged in all aspects of the Museum, from curatorial roles to policy making.
www.abbemuseum.org

BEECH HILL FARM

College of the Atlantic's Beech Hill Farm is a working farm growing fresh vegetables and raising meat for COA and the wider community. Collaborative work and planning between Beech Hill Farm and the kitchen is helping COA to "close the loop," forming a more sustainable system of food production and consumption. Beech Hill Farm operates a seasonal farm stand, offers a CSA program, and sells to local markets and restaurants.
www.coa.edu/farms/beech-hill-farm/

FRIENDS OF ACADIA

Friends of Acadia members make possible essential conservation projects in Acadia National Park and the surrounding communities.
www.friendsofacadia.org

JESUP MEMORIAL LIBRARY

The Jesup Memorial Library is a community resource and gathering place.
www.jesuplibrary.org

MOUNT DESERT ISLAND HISTORICAL SOCIETY

Our mission is to foster meaningful engagement with the histories of Mount Desert Island.
www.mdihistory.org

SOUTHWEST HARBOR LIBRARY

To be the place where people of all ages and backgrounds come to improve literacy, explore new ideas, and pursue lifelong learning interests.
www.swhplibrary.org

Great Smoky Mountains National Park

FRIENDS OF THE BLUE RIDGE PARKWAY—ROANOKE, VA, CHAPTER

Roanoke Valley's volunteers help to preserve, promote and enhance the Blue Ridge Parkway as it winds through the Plateau District of southern Virginia.
www.friendsbrp.org/who-we-are/chapters /roanoke-valley-chapter-2

FRIENDS OF THE SMOKIES

Friends of Great Smoky Mountains National Park assists the National Park Service in its mission to preserve and protect Great Smoky Mountains National Park by raising funds and public awareness, and providing volunteers for needed projects.

www.friendsofthesmokies.org

GREAT SMOKY MOUNTAINS ASSOCIATION

Great Smoky Mountains Association supports the perpetual preservation of Great Smoky Mountains National Park and the national park system by promoting greater public interest and appreciation through education, interpretation, and research.

www.smokiesinformation.org

MUSEUM OF THE CHEROKEE INDIAN

Located in Cherokee, NC, the Museum of the Cherokee Indian strives to perpetuate the history, culture, & stories of the Cherokee people.

www.cherokeemuseum.org

Rocky Mountain National Park

ROCKY MOUNTAIN CONSERVANCY

Founded in 1931, the Rocky Mountain Conservancy (formerly the Rocky Mountain Nature Association) is a nonprofit organization supporting Rocky Mountain National Park. When you support the Conservancy, you're supporting one of our national treasures for generations to come.

www.rmconservancy.org

YMCA OF THE ROCKIES

YMCA of the Rockies, located near the town of Estes Park and Rocky Mountain National Park, is an ideal vacation, reunion, wedding, and conference destination.

www.ymcarockies.org

Zion National Park

ZION CANYON FIELD INSTITUTE

The Zion Canyon Field Institute educates and inspires local, national, and international visitors to the greater Zion National Park ecosystem and environment through intensive classes that immerse visitors in the field.

www.zionpark.org/classes

ZION NATURAL HISTORY ASSOCIATION

Zion Natural History Association (ZNHA) was established in 1929 to support education, research, publication, and other programs for the benefit of Zion National Park, Cedar Breaks National Monument, and Pipe Spring National Monument. Bookstore sales, as well as support from members and contributors, combine to provide the parks with more than $600,000 in aid annually.

www.zionpark.org

Yosemite National Park

MARIPOSA COUNTY LIBRARY

The Mariposa County Library System is committed to supporting lifelong learning and knowledge through self-education for all the residents and visitors of Mariposa County. The Library strives to enrich the lives of all users by meeting the informational, recreational, self-educational and cultural needs of the community.

www.mariposalibrary.org

MARIPOSA MUSEUM & HISTORY CENTER

Founded in 1957, the museum's mission is to authentically portray the people and lifestyle of Mariposa County from the Native American and Spanish periods to the California Gold Rush and through the early 1900s.
ww.mariposamuseum.com

NATUREBRIDGE

NatureBridge provides hands-on environmental science programs for children and teens. Our multi-day programs take place outdoors in the magnificence of nature's classroom, where students are immersed in the wonder and science of our national parks including Yosemite.
www.naturebridge.org

YOSEMITE CONSERVANCY

Yosemite Conservancy provides grants to Yosemite National Park based on the highest-priority needs of the park. It has funded the restoration of the trail to Lower Yosemite Falls, electronic bear-monitoring equipment to keep bears safe, life-changing youth programs, and much more.
www.yosemiteconservancy.org

Yellowstone National Park

YELLOWSTONE FOREVER

The nonprofit Yellowstone Forever is building a new model of partnership with the National Park Service, one that will engage more visitors and future stewards than ever before. The opportunities that Yellowstone Forever provides—to experience, connect, and contribute—are the first steps in a lifelong journey for people who want to preserve the park for generations to come.
www.yellowstone.org

YELLOWSTONE FOREVER INSTITUTE

The Yellowstone Forever Institute introduces thousands of students to the park's natural wonders. Programs range from one day to three weeks in length, and highlight the park's amazing wildlife, geothermal areas, rich history, and awe-inspiring wilderness.
www.yellowstone.org/experience /yellowstone-forever-institute

YELLOWSTONE GATEWAY MUSEUM

The Yellowstone Gateway Museum of Park County's mission is to collect, preserve, and interpret the cultural and natural history of Park County, Montana and its relationship to Yellowstone Park for the education of everyone.
www.yellowstonegatewaymuseum.org

YELLOWSTONE RESEARCH LIBRARY

The mission of the Yellowstone Research Library is to collect published and unpublished materials related to Yellowstone and to make these materials available to park staff, researchers, and the general public. The library collection consists of more than 20,000 books, periodicals, theses and dissertations, unpublished manuscripts, microforms of historic newspapers and scrapbooks, brochures, technical reports, and audio visual material.
www.nps.gov/yell/learn/historyculture/library.htm

About the Editors

Dave Kyu is a socially engaged artist and writer. Born in Seoul, South Korea, and raised in the United States, his work explores the creative tensions of identity, community, and public space. He has made public art in collaboration with local communities for the Mural Arts Program, Asian Arts Initiative, and the City of Philadelphia. His own creative projects have found him commissioning skywriting planes to create messages 10,000 feet over Philadelphia, and doing everything Facebook told him to do for a month. His writing has been published in *Generocity*, the *Artblog*, and the *Philadelphia Citizen*.

 Ilyssa Kyu is a designer and strategist. She received a bachelor of science in industrial design from the University of the Arts in Philadelphia. Ilyssa's

human-centered design approach helps individuals and organizations further their impact in the world by finding opportunities and clarity in the chaos as well as unconventional, creative ways of solving problems. She has worked as a designer at the Office of Sustainability for the City of Philadelphia and design studios including andCulture and P'unk Avenue. She is interested in exploring her role as a design strategist to support outdoor and wildlife conservation organizations.

Sean Shapiro

About the Illustrators

ACADIA NATIONAL PARK ILLUSTRATION

Allison May Kiphuth

www.allisonmaykiphuth.com/portfolio

GREAT SMOKY MOUNTAINS NATIONAL PARK ILLUSTRATION

Sarah Jacoby

www.thesarahjacoby.com

ROCKY MOUNTAINS NATIONAL PARK ILLUSTRATION

Emily Dove

www.emilydove.com

ZION NATIONAL PARK ILLUSTRATION

Maggie Chiang

www.hellomaggiec.com

YOSEMITE NATIONAL PARK ILLUSTRATION

Josie Portillo

www.portilloillustration.com

YELLOWSTONE NATIONAL PARK ILLUSTRATION

Zoe Keller

www.zoekeller.com

MOUNTAINEERS BOOKS is a leading publisher of mountaineering literature and guides— including our flagship title, *Mountaineering: The Freedom of the Hills*—as well as adventure narratives, natural history, and general outdoor recreation. Through our two imprints, Skipstone and Braided River, we also publish titles on sustainability and conservation. We are committed to supporting the environmental and educational goals of our organization by providing expert information on human-powered adventure, sustainable practices at home and on the trail, and preservation of wilderness.

The Mountaineers, founded in 1906, is a 501(c)(3) nonprofit outdoor recreation and conservation organization whose mission is to enrich lives and communities by helping people "explore, conserve, learn about, and enjoy the lands and waters of the Pacific Northwest and beyond." One of the largest such organizations in the United States, it sponsors classes and year-round outdoor activities throughout the Pacific Northwest, including climbing, hiking, backcountry skiing, snowshoeing, camping, kayaking, sailing, and more. The Mountaineers also supports its mission through its publishing division, Mountaineers Books, and promotes environmental education and citizen engagement. For more information, visit The Mountaineers Program Center, 7700 Sand Point Way NE, Seattle, WA 98115-3996; phone 206-521-6001; www.mountaineers.org; or email info@mountaineers.org.

Our publications are made possible through the generosity of donors and through sales of more than 800 titles on outdoor recreation, sustainable lifestyle, and conservation. To donate, purchase books, or learn more, visit us online:

MOUNTAINEERS BOOKS

1001 SW Klickitat Way, Suite 201 • Seattle, WA 98134

800-553-4453 • mbooks@mountaineersbooks.org • www.mountaineersbooks.org

More from Mountaineers Books

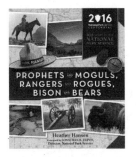

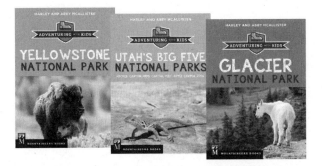

Prophets and Moguls, Rangers and Rogues, Bison and Bears

Heather Hansen

An engaging and accessible account of the first one hundred years of the National Park Service

Yellowstone National Park: Adventuring with Kids

Utah's Big Five National Parks: Adventuring with Kids

Glacier National Park: Adventuring with Kids

Harley and Abby McAllister

Three great guidebooks that cover seven national parks in the West: perfect for busy families planning their own national park adventures

The Adventure Gap

James Mills

Expedition Denali and its team members' adventures are a jumping-off point to share the stories of minorities who have achieved significant accomplishments in the outdoors.

The Pacific Crest Trailside Reader: California

The Pacific Crest Trailside Reader: Oregon and Washington

Rees Hughes and Corey Lewis, editors

Real trail tales about the Pacific Crest Trail, ranging from classic historical accounts to modern-day hikers' stories

www.mountaineersbooks.org